Lady Victoria Welby

Grains of Sense

GRAINS OF SENSE

BY

V. WELBY

"After all, there is a grain of sense in it."—*Popular remark*

If the title seems to claim too much, let the reader say how less could well be claimed than the sense which is not only reason, but also the barest meaning which words can give. If a thing don't stand to reason,
at least it must kneel to sense.

LONDON
J. M. DENT & CO.
67 S. JAMES'S STREET, S.W
1897

Lady Victoria Welby

Grains of Sense

ISBN/EAN: 9783744679183

Printed in Europe, USA, Canada, Australia, Japan

Cover: Foto ©Thomas Meinert / pixelio.de

More available books at **www.hansebooks.com**

DEDICATED

TO

THE MISUNDERSTOOD

SECTIONS

Parable: The Clearer.
- 1-3. An urgent need.
- 4. The wise writer.
- 5, 6. Law and lucidity.
- 7-9. Sign and Sense.
- 10, 11. Sir G. C. Lewis and "Lewis Carroll".
- 12. Sir J. Seeley's "delight".
- 13-15. Savagery in Language.
- 16. A Linguistic Intelligence Department.
- 17. A new Journalism.
- 18, 19. Short-tongue: unicode: logotype.
- 20-22. Prof. Flinders Petrie's crusade against writing: *Times* and *Punch* on this.
- 23, 24. Mr Leslie Stephen on "accumulation".
- 25, 26. Mislocution.
- 27. The signs of awakening.
- 28, 29. "Clearing the air".
- 30. Education.
- 31. Illustration.
- 32, 33. The deaf-mute.
- 34. Prof. Mahaffy's "Modern Babel".
- 35. Mr H. Spencer on Gesture-language.
- 36. A composite Glossary.
- 37. Prof. Mahaffy's appeal.
- 38. Bishop Wilkins' Philosophical Language.
- 39-43. Spelling: its vagaries and its tyranny.
- 44. Mr Chamberlain on Meaning.

45, 46. Prof. W. Raleigh on words.
47. Prof. Croom Robertson on malapropism.
48. Misused words.
49. Cobbett's Political Grammar.
50-52. Language as she is spoke.
53. Handles and spouts.
54. The Farmer and his boy.
55. The Overseer of Evolution.
56. Losing senses.
57. Mr Smith and Mr Brown.
58. The breeze of dawn.
59. The *Athenæum* on L. Housman's diction.
60, 61. The Inexpressible.
62. The Word.
63, 64. Limitations.
65. Mind and Speech.
66. Incoherent Development.
67. Mr J. Morley on French synonyms.
68. R. L. Stevenson on Fleeming Jenkin.
69. Hobbes.
70. Speech and gesture: Mrs Meynell.
71. A world of view.
72. An International Court of Appeal.
73. The Seer succeeded by the Critic.
74. The Medicine-Man replaced by the Meaning-Man.
75. Ennius, Lucretius, Cicero, Virgil, as Makers of Speech.
76. Linguistic developments in India and Japan.
77. An appeal for united effort.
78. The Sententious and the Prig.
79. Dr Weir Mitchell's experiment and Nansen on the Eskimo.
80, 81. Light and its meaning.
82. Sound money and Free silver.
83. Mr Morley's " salt ".

84. Metaphors of Consciousness.
85-87. Bulls.
88. The Schoolmaster—at sea.
89. A figurative Conscience.
90-93. Literal Absurdities.

PARABLES

Eye the Mystic.
The Animal Critics.
Interviewing an Impassable Gulf.
" So-to-speak ", and " As-it-were ".
How to stand Upright
Changing Views.
The Evolution of Heliology.

FINAL NOTE

THE CLEARER.

THE Talker and the Writer went off arm in arm in a great fuss—they often are in a great fuss—to consult the Wiseacre about the messes they were always getting into. "Here I've got three law-suits on my hands", said the Writer; "and my lawyer declares he can't define one of the terms on which they turn, so they'll probably last a lifetime and cost a fortune".

"And I've made ten new enemies by the speeches I made to clear the air", answered the Talker; "and they threaten to ruin my career, while one of the papers says I mean black and another says I mean white".

"Do you think after all", said the Writer thoughtfully, "that the Wiseacre *is* the best person to go to? He never seems to have anything fresh to say: he only looks solemn and it's always, in pompous accents, 'Take care of the thoughts and the words will take care of themselves', or else, 'Whatever you do use plain words with plain meaning that nobody can possibly contrive to mistake'. And then we go and try, and we find that it's rather the other way up: take care of the words or you'll find that the thoughts are not worth speaking of, and sometimes the plainer the words the less plain the meaning: while you must have a poor opinion of your fellow-creatures if you think they can't contrive to mistake whatever you say. O dear, there seems only one motto for language or its dictionaries and grammars and spelling, and that's ' Confusion worse confounded ' ".

"Well", replied the Talker, "I believe there is another Adviser round the corner; suppose we try him? They say he keeps some sort of tabloid or pilule which, when you swallow it, really does clear up everything. Anyhow, he can't be a worse quack than the Wiseacre, and I never heard that he advertised or got money out of anyone". "What's his name"? asked the Writer. "I never heard that", answered the Talker. "I fancy he don't care for calling names, or for those that most of us give or bear". "No wonder", returned the Talker laughing: "what we call a thing is often exactly what it isn't". At this moment they found themselves at an unassuming little door with these words over it :—

The Clearer.

Whoever wants to make the most of his words may knock here. No charge.

So they knocked and were admitted. When they had explained their trouble and their wishes, their host put his hand into a small bag on the table and pulled out a very tiny round thing which they could hardly see. Holding this with his thumb and finger he said, "Here, my friends, is the only thing I know of that can help you. Take this, which is one single Grain of Sense. Apply it vigorously to all the questions of language, rub it well on every page of the dictionary, touch the alphabet with it and soak all the grammar books in some water in which you have boiled it, and you will find they will all begin to change very much for the better. Then swallow it yourself and it will begin to work inside you till you feel a glow of meaning and 'reasons why' spread over everything, and things which now seem impossible will turn out quite feasible. You will find, like the girl in the fairy tale, that instead of the slugs or adders, or the bits of fluff and waste that used to flow from your mouth or pen, now there drop pearls and diamonds and all manner of precious things, throwing light upon whatever they touch. But though you are welcome to my poor little grain, remember that my own store of them is very scanty. When they multiply a hundred-fold, as they do in the right mouths and pens—which of course are yours!—please remember to send me back a few to keep my own little bag full". So the friends promised they would, and went away together. "But after all", said the one to the other, "now we come to think of it, a grain of sense is a very common thing; and we might have picked it up by the roadside and left the man with the little bag alone. Anyhow let us try his plan and see what comes of it".

All references will be found at the end of the book.

. . . 1 . . .

If " we are none of us infallible, not even the youngest ", it is also true that we are all of us ambiguous, even the eldest.

. . . 2 . . .

If a little knowledge is dangerous, much is fatal: and indeed at a trial experts usually contradict each other and often in good faith. What we want is not so much more knowledge as more interpretation of what we already have, and enhanced powers of symbolising it.

. . . 3 . . .

It is surely time we applied to all means of expression and communication the elementary truth that man *is* man in so far as he can use for his own ends the " raw material " of Nature; in so far as he voluntarily directs and controls both "himself" and the "not-self" for intelligent ends. We ought to be simply ashamed of our toleration of the prevalent helplessness: of the chaos in which we still leave expression: of the hap-hazard developments of language. We have enormously developed all means of communication *except the most important of all.*

. . . 4 . . .

As things are it often takes a wise writer to read his own writing: perhaps it takes a still wiser one to read his own meaning.

. . . 5 . . .

For instance, the Law, exactly the case in which at great cost we are supposed to secure the most rigorous definition, conspicuously fails to read its own meaning. The *Daily Graphic*[1] is quite justified in saying that "to an intelligent foreigner the spectacle of five judges, with the help of some of the leading lights of the Bar, one of whom has occupied the position of a Secretary of State, solemnly trying to make up their minds as to what constitutes a 'place', would be productive of open-eyed and perhaps even contemptuous wonder"; especially if besides that, he heard an eminent lawyer say, "I

Grains of Sense

declined, my lord, just now to define a house, and I must also decline to define a structure". The only definition satisfactorily arrived at on this occasion seems to be that of a welsher by Mr Justice Hawkins, as a man who is present in the morning and absent in the afternoon.

. . .   6   . . .

But the law also perversely keeps up distinctions which have ceased to have any value and are actually misleading ; for instance, that between the sentence of imprisonment and the sentence of penal servitude. The term " hard " added to labour " has no particular meaning, and its employment in the sentence makes no practical difference ".[2] When will a linguistic conscience begin to prick us and insist upon more respect for Sense ?

. . .   7   . . .

Sense ? What is Sense and what do we mean by it ? Seeing and hearing and smelling and touching ? Or what belongs to words and phrases ? Or the quality which we so value in each other when we say with relief, that is a man of sense, that was a sensible thing to do, I can see the sense of that ? Or that subtle thing which we call the sense of a meeting, the sense of disapproval, the sense of duty, the religious or philosophical sense of an age or race? When this question was first put, a protest was raised against there being any traceable connection between the "sense of touch" and the "sense of a word". Now it has been shown by Dr Murray that such a connection probably exists. So when we ask what Sense is, there may be some new answers to be given. We want men of sense in a new sense.

. . . 8 . . .

The worm wasn't content even with building his world. He wanted to see it; and he grew eyes and gave his world an inverted image. Then he grew a little Sense and put some in his world. So he became a Man. And he filled his world with signs and symbols and knew that it was Significant. But it was a long time before his man-self learnt the lesson of the ancestral worm-self and found out how little we know, how much we can do if we try —and all try together—and how many worlds as we climb and climb we may learn to see and to interpret. And unhappily he meanwhile invented non-sense. So it was longer still before he found out,—what like M. Jourdain he had been acting upon all his life—the fact that nothing *signifies* except what really signifies—the Sign : and that Sense alone gives this and is its value too. The Sense of Sign follows the Sign of Sense.

. . .   9   . . .

Some would tell us that in this world we are saved by our want of faith; but it is perhaps more certain that we are lost by our want of sense. Walpole's epigram, "don't read me history, for I know that can't be true", might be applied much more widely as long as we ignore the difficulties of " meaning ".

. . .   10   . . .

While we are rightly warned by writers like Sir G. C. Lewis[3] that "verbal" ambiguities poison the whole current of our reasoning and " vitiate every part which they touch ", and that " not even those who know the ambiguity of a term are always proof against the confusion which it tends to generate "; while, as Mr Holyoake points out,[4] "persons whom you take to be wise and are bound to think honest, will arrest discussion and conceal their own ignorance by insisting that the point in dispute is a mere affair of terms", it is strange indeed to find Huxley himself saying[5] that "it really matters very little in what sense terms are used, so long as the same meaning is always rigidly attached to them": as if it was possible to secure such rigid attachment, especially in the very cases where perfect fitness is most needed.

.   .   .   11   .   .   .

Quite as strange is the position taken by Lewis Carroll in his Symbolic Logic [6]:—"I maintain that any writer of a book is fully authorised in attaching any meaning he likes to any word or phrase he intends to use. If I find an author saying, at the beginning of his book, 'Let it be understood that by the word "*black*" I shall always mean "*white*" and that by the word "*white*" I shall always mean "*black*", I meekly accept his ruling, however injudicious I may think it'". A letter to him on this principle would of course seem merely a bad imitation of the missives in Wonderland: but perhaps if a member of the House were to announce before speaking that he intended to use the words liar, thief, scoundrel, and traitor in a complimentary sense, the Speaker might find

Grains of Sense

some difficulty in meekly accepting his definitions. The Queen's Speech again is the proverbial butt of the purist, sometimes perhaps even of the common-sense man; but at least we meekly accept and make the best of it, which we, or our foreign friends, would hardly do if advantage were taken of Lewis Carroll's rule, and the Queen was made to announce " hostile measures" which had previously been defined as " friendly overtures " with reference to foreign powers.

It is amazing that a prince of humourists like Lewis Carroll should fail to see that such a practice, become common, would strike at the heart of humour itself: and should also overlook the tremendous part that associations called up by terms and phrases play in the effect of his Wonderland books. We might define till we were hoarse: the author might have begun ' Alice' with a chapter in large capitals, thus.

In this book :—

Alice	shall mean	Punch.
Sitting	,, ,,	squeaking.
White Rabbit	,,	Black Pig.
Cats	,, ,,	Pots.
Bats	,, ,,	Pans.
The Dodo	,,	The Coalscuttle.

And so on all through the book. Or in the Symbolic Logic itself he might have begun by announcing that

 Proposition shall mean Fallacy.
 Syllogism ,, ,, Contradiction.
and so on. But it is to be feared that the result would be repudiated alike by young and old readers, with anything but meekness.

At this rate indeed, our motto will be, Every man his own Dictionary. And we shall have to revise our opinion of the famous game, "When I say hold fast, let go; When I say let go, hold fast". Instead of expecting and enjoying the resulting chaos, and the desperate efforts of the players to untie the hard knots of association, we shall treat it as a valuable example of the legitimate prerogatives of the definer.

  . . . 12 . . .

It has been said of Sir J. Seeley[7] that "he delights in packing a century into a formula, a policy into a paradox, a career into a phrase". That means, as the writer truly adds, a singular power of simplifying the complex and giving us its main features. But more. It means a concentration of sense. Why should not every child be brought up on the axiom that the first, second and third need in language is a common sense and a special sense; to expect a common consent in *con-sense* that we are to combine in looking for and adopting first the most adequate, and secondly the most economical form of expression, just as we do in all other matters?

. . .   13   . . .

When we wandered in primeval forests in the days before we spoke, we lived only to eat and drink and to take care of the little ones; but now that we have grown wise and grand and think and talk and criticise,—do we leave off eating and drinking and taking care of the little ones? No; but we learn why we should and how much may come of the life we nourish and cherish. We learn that what was *end* to us once becomes *means* now: what stood *in* our way as a final object becomes our way; the road to higher things. So with the highest Way, we find it in leaving it behind; necessarily in rightly using it, passing beyond it. If we take our stand upon our way, making it a fixed dwelling-place, we lose it and deny it in the act. The sense, the value of the metaphor is lost. In how many cases is this true? But perhaps we are still at an early stage. We may approve only of things which "run on all fours" with each other. Nature means them to become biped. But in learning that, they sway a little at first; and we think them tipsy or idiotic! Again, more sense is wanted in our "way of putting things".

Or let us go further back still. We're all, it may be, rooted;—stuck fast in the ground: Mind-plants: we are proud of being impossible to move. But what if we must needs be plucked up and torn away,—and learn to move with no "support" like the world we live on? What indeed if our solid common-sense has to be swung out into the boundless gulfs of vagueness, to learn its place—its lack of place rather; its pace and trackless journey? Well "others too, being men, have borne things which had to be endured"; and common-sense might come back to us from such an experience, having learnt a little more of what it might mean, and how far from common its higher forms yet are.

.   .   .   14   .   .   .

Or again, we may say that in the all-important matter of expression we are like a mere horde of savages wandering over jungles and prairies, gathering nuts or edible weeds as we happen to

Grains of Sense

find them, and devouring animals raw. The expression-horde which lives from "hand to mouth" (successors of paw and maw) and has not even the orderly coherence of a flock of geese or a shoal of herrings or a pack of wolves, protests that nothing better can be hoped for, and that civilisation of *whatever* type is impossible, or if possible undesirable, as destroying freedom and mechanising life. What is the result of this attitude? The linguistic Bushman: the lowest human type. And be it noted that it is exactly the Bushman, who by his remarkable artistic exploits, shows that he both has and could use profitably the "higher" powers which he leaves undeveloped. So with the "Bushman" of language, which Man is still content to be. In this sense, assuredly, "the primitive Aryan is with us now".[8]

. . . 15 . . .

And if it be true, as according to M. Piette [9] there seems reasonable ground for believing, that even the Neolithic troglodytes had arrived at "numerals, symbols, pictographic signs", if not actual "alphabetical characters", it certainly seems high time that we emerged from a linguistic impotence of which the troglodyte himself might have been relatively ashamed.

. . . 16 . . .

Do we care for art, for science, for philosophy, for religion,—for the solutions of social or "economical" problems? Are we poets or mathematicians, musicians or astronomers, painters or tradesmen, missioners or manufacturers, philosophers or politicians, novelists or journalists or explorers? In every case the first need is to develop immensely the power of Communication between " mind " and " mind ": the power of Expression of all that passes or grows in " mind ": and the corresponding power of interpreting, understanding and finally *translating* expression of every kind and of every degree of complexity and subtlety. Thus we get to the idea of a sort of " Staff College ": to a spider's web of Mutual Interpretation with lines running in every direction; and to an " Intelligence Department" of the human army. We want to train the Messenger, the Scout, the Patrol, the " look-out man". But the man whose duty it is to keep us in intellectual touch with each other and with what is passing beyond the intellectual camp, must not be expected to do anything else or more.

. . . 17 . . .

To vary the metaphor, or rather to apply another analogy, we want another Press; we want a journalism of expression itself; not the newspaper, but its human analogue, the human gazette; the man whose main duty begins and ends in " news ", and who, at most, can but add to this a brief and general comment upon it. Let us catch the scout-mind early and press its gifts into the general service. Let us throw out human outposts on every side, let us create new human " organs of intelligence " in two senses. And thus let us utilise the " versatile " man, and turn the " mystic " into the Signal-man and the Pioneer. How we waste our dreamers, our fanatics, our cranks! As in life-saving apparatus so in knowledge-bringing apparatus. You must attach a rope to the rocket, and must not abuse the head because it can only explode and can never pull in. At present we idly waste the human rockets, or leave them to amuse a holiday crowd. Well, indeed, if they don't set fire to something that we value! At present who knows how many charlatans, and even intellectual and moral pirates and buccaneers are the morbid product of our neglect to use and direct urgent vital energies? We do encourage geographical explorers; let us extend the conception and encourage explorers of the expression-world, sending out well equipped expeditions into the polar regions of Meaning. And let us have endless "liners" from one intellectual continent to another; endless "cables" across every intellectual ocean, as we already have endless telescopic minds trained upon the starry depths of ether and endless microscopic ones fixed upon the worlds within a speck.

. . . 18 . . .

Again, let us have laboratories of experimental language. Let us test, in many ways, the quantity and quality of the sense of meaning. Let us try experiments in this on new lines. Let us utilise gifts which are now little more than curiosities for exhibition; the 8-game blindfold chess-players, the "great calculators", the intellectual acrobats and conjurors generally.

. . . 19 . . .

We already have shorthand; we want short-tongue and short-mind; we want a much larger proportion of meaning to expression. Then we may hope for a larger proportion of sense to meaning, and of significance to sense, bringing out untold treasures now buried in dumbness and, as we are, unspeakable. We already say, "one look was enough", and, indeed, in many ways, even savage gesture is still ahead of language, as the orator discovers. We want more alphabets and fewer long and fearsome words, unless these are concentrated paragraphs (as they sometimes are in German). Let us apply the principle of economy in ordinary language as we do apply it in technical notation and in "unicodes" and "logotypes", though, of course, not in the same forms or methods; rather in the actor's, by studying the expression-effect of every slightest movement or attitude.

. . .   20   . . .

If we complain that to apply the principle of the unicode to scientific or philosophical writing would be sacrificing instead of cultivating delicate shades of "meaning", we must remember that what is here urged as wanted, is really a further application of the principle of the Alphabet itself. Only Professor Flinders Petrie,[10] it may be supposed, would deny that the acquisition of the alphabet has been, to the human race, the opening of a teeming mine of mental wealth; or attempt to suggest that this has not merely blunted a precious keenness of sense, dimmed the eye and numbed the hand of the artist-nature, but that "the true place of writing", is merely for "registering details that are too many for the mind to carry, or for rapid and distant communication": that "its real place is by the side of the railway and the telegraph; things that do not add the least to the nature of the mind, but are mere tools imposed upon us by the need of not being outstripped by those who use them". Strange, indeed, that one who owes so much, as this very address shows, to the power of expressing complex and abstract thought which writing alone preserves to us and enables us to accumulate, should be so unconscious of it, and so ready to fling away the highest mental tool we have. But, indeed, his protest may well be read in the light of a discontent with the results of our endless scribbling which ought to give us some better remedy than the abolition of writing itself. There is a sense in which it is well to be reminded that we are "drunken with writing": that we "let it override the growth of our minds and the common use of our senses. When first the power of speech in ruling man was felt, the servant speech was soon mistaken for the master thought". But if speech were worthier, it would more fully justify Wordsworth's saying, that language is the incarnation of thought, and would tend to restore lost powers and lost touch with nature. It would be in more vital touch with the realities of life.

. . .   21   . . .

In its comment on the address, the *Times*[11] admits that as things are, too many of us have never learned to attach precise meanings to words learnt; and declares that "the good effects of what is called education in the present day are to a great extent neutralised by the careless views which prevail, among teachers as well as among the taught, with regard to the meaning of words which are in common use". And so the language written as well as spoken which might and ought to be a pure boon to mankind "is squandered over trivialities, until the common scribe has nothing left for the purposes of accurate description or of enduring record. And it is just because the majority of people use words without knowing or caring what they mean, that they become, under certain conditions, such powerful agencies for working mischief". Well, may it be added, "How many political catchwords have possessed this character, owing their power for evil to the fact that they were calculated to excite, in the minds of the unreasoning majority of the public, ideas which would have been refuted if they had been openly and clearly expressed! It would not be difficult to find, among the young men and women of the present day, large numbers who are said, and supposed, to be educated, but who in reality know nothing, because they do not know any language with sufficient accuracy to permit them to form and to impart definite ideas. One of South's most striking sermons is on 'The terrible imposture and force of words;' and it is to these qualities of words, for the most part artificially bestowed by carelessness, that the mental slavery from which Professor Petrie desires to deliver us seems, so far as it is real, for the most part to be attributable".

These are wise and weighty words. Would that they could bear speedy fruit!

. . . 22 . . .

With apologies to Mr Punch [12] we may quote some words both wise and witty on the same address:—

"Drunken with writing? Aye, Sir, and dys-
    peptic,
Hysterical, insane, and epileptic
    With sheer excess of scribble!
'Tis words, words, words, in plenteous printer's
    ink,
Make man a thing that never thinks to think,
    A phrase-devouring fribble.

The Parliament, the Platform, Pulpit, Press,
Pack us with words, and yet we make a mess
    Of most things that need *thinking*.
We suck up speech as sands suck water up,
And yet compare as Hamlet with a Krupp,
    From 'name of action' shrinking.

A crowd of geese, we cackle, cackle, cackle,
But when Fate gives some Gordian knot to tackle,
    Still wordily we wrangle.
A multitude of talkers all unstable,
Confronted with a knot they are unable
    To cut or disentangle.

. . . .

> Ins and Outs
> Exchange wild eloquence in windy flouts,
>   And papers print the lot of it;
> We word-devourers read and call it grand,
> All unaware we do not understand
>   The stale sophistic rot of it".

. . . 23 . . .

And how can we hope to become aware that we are the victims of " stale sophistic rot " while we think it can't matter except for the pedant, the pedagogue, or even the prig, whether we make the most or the least of language: even whether we talk of meaning or of sense or of import or of significance, or what these distinctions are worth? How can we wonder that we " make a mess of most things that need thinking " as long as we are impatient at the very idea that there is anything that *signifies* to be learnt about signifying? What in the world does it signify? we cry, and so close the discussion—by giving ourselves away. But some day perhaps we shall be taught from our childhood that what signifies more than anything is that true significance which is the whole and sole value of life and of all that it brings to Man the Master of meaning, Man the Autocrat of sense, who is yet a wretched slave—to his own poor and crude and barbarous Expression. Some day perhaps it will dawn upon us that the endless complaints and lamentations about the failure of language to express *this*, the tendency of language to confuse *that*, the tremendous power for good or harm which a word or phrase has over us : the constant mutual accusations of misrepresenting, misapprehending, misreading, misunderstanding ; have, if as yet no conscious intention, at least a profound and practical significance. Perhaps further it will even dawn upon us that it is mostly a needless and cruel waste ; that if we had made up our minds that we could never hope to write, we never should have written; that it is largely our taking for granted that language cannot be raised to a higher level and become more expressive which causes our bondage to its barbarisms ; and that, once we make up our minds that we intend to be masters and not abject serfs of our speech —the most "intelligent" and "voluntary" of all organic activities,—a most wonderful and undreamt-of change will begin. Slowly we may learn to realise that a generation specially trained to express and to translate expression, to expect more expression-power, to work in every language to this end: trained to signify more and to interpret better, will even thus have gone a long way towards healing the cruel "misunderstandings" which divide us in mutual suspicion and even hostility, or at least paralyse our mental action; and which help to poison with unreality, our highest and truest ideals. A generation thus educated,—thus "brought up" —will begin to see solutions of familiar problems which, as we are, are indeed beyond the hope of the wildest optimist; and will have, at first silently and tentatively, then articulately and definitely, started on one of the greatest advances which the human race has ever made,— *an advance in the power of mental inter-communication.*

. . . 24 . . .

Leslie Stephen tells us [13] that the "gigantic increase in the power of man over nature" which we call civilization (or progress) is due to the one fact that man can *accumulate.* He can store up and hand on from generation to generation not only tools but knowledge—not only of facts but of scientific laws and methods of investigation. Thus "the dwarf now stands on the shoulders of the giant". Yes: and a gigantic increase in the power of man over all forms of mental communication will depend again on this power to accumulate. It must be hoped that we shall not much longer, as we now do, idly let go of really valuable words painfully acquired by our forefathers, and look upon them as merely archaic or merely quaint; but hand them on as "tools" for our children. We have only to look at our Bible and our Shakespeare to be assured of the present waste.

He tells us again that thanks to the accumulating power, the average undergraduate now solves with ease, problems which once baffled the greatest intellects. So also now there are classes of problems—among the most important for human welfare that exist—which still puzzle the greatest intellects among us, but which, when we seriously apply ourselves to develop language in its widest sense *as we have developed other powers*, will in their turn and in the same sense be "solved with ease" by the "average undergraduate".

We are reminded also that certain stages of intellectual progress are "abnormally stimulating"; that, "as the last step to a pass in the mountains suddenly reveals vast prospects, while a hundred equally difficult steps before made no appreciable change, so there are mental advances which, as at the time of Bacon, seemed nearly to disclose boundless prospects of knowledge ". Are we arrived at or nearing such a stage now? Will not the idea of acquiring more worthy—nobler—modes of expression act as such a stimulus? Most surely the least that can be said of words is that they are Thought heard and seen. And it would be well to make up our minds that the thought, which we suppose to be too high for words, will generally on examination, be found to be *lower* than words,—to belong, that is, to the inarticulate " feeling " which we share with the " dumb animal ". Thought, however, may well in another sense be unspeakable in our present modes of speech and really too high for them, but if so it is predictive at least of the speech which we may have, if we will it and work for it, and train our children to command and acquire it; which will come in proportion as we learn to realise our power to bring it forth, and to control and utilise it to the utmost. Only, once more, let us remember that, as with other forms of power which belong to man's advance, what we now call " words " or " language ", may, and indeed must, become an altogether richer and more powerful means of mutual understanding than anything we yet possess. When we say that first-rate writing " is clear because it is thorough, not because it is shallow ", we point to the direction in which our hopes should tend. Average writing among intelligent men might become more thorough than it is. If it can be truly said that the average undergraduate now solves with ease problems which once baffled the greatest intellects : if, *e.g.*, the Copernican view of the sun and the Newtonian principle of gravitation are now the general possession, while inventions which once required exceptional genius to deal with them are now worked by the ordinary artisan, most certainly we may look for the same result in what problems and inventions first require—the power to be adequately, clearly, simply, thoroughly *expressed*.

. . . 25 . . .

We are absurdly inconsistent in this matter. We all agree that our children have got to learn to read and write. So we establish a consensus on the alphabet and all which follows from it, sufficient at least for this purpose. We call out voluntary effort in this direction,—

and the result is, well, at least, the difference between the savage and the civilized man. Having made up our minds that we will all read and write, we both create and accumulate mental treasure, and make rationally acquired knowledge possible and accessible. Let us then extend the same principle to that which alone gives a trace of value to reading or writing. After all, it is agreed among experts that the eye and the ear could be trained and educated to a much higher power than they now possess.[14] And that would be useless without a corresponding rise in the power to interpret, and to express clearly and fully what we perceived and inferred. As things are, to " sense " more without a real linguistic advance would be merely to increase the area of existing confusion, and produce fresh denunciations of that impotence of language which is the result of our failure to realise on the one hand our own tremendous power over it, and on the other, while this lies unused, its disastrous power over us. Let us see then that our children may realise this: may understand that the present condition of language is little more than elementary, while, if they will, its future may be illimitable.

. . . 26 . . .

It is no answer to point to existing examples of what we call "lucidity", mastery of language, command of literary style, since these practically correspond to the self-taught musician or painter: an orator or writer is "lucid" by natural gift which has had no direct, though no doubt much indirect, cultivation. It is still less an answer to remind us of possible remedy in a rigid technical notation, an "exact" and "precise" form of expression; since this is both fatally to crush a living organism into an unyielding mould, and to be in fact occult and useless to all but a small section of minds and a small range of subjects. For what we want is more adequate forms of expression for every need of humanity; for every mode of mental activity, for every type of experience, for every world of possible knowledge and possible feeling, and possible willing and acting. With this must go more adequate powers of interpretation, making possible more thorough assimilation of delicate complexities of significance, and greater sensitiveness to its ceaseless changes and expansions. Why cannot we see that *mislocution* is speech halt and maimed and palsied; that the misspoken is less tolerable than the misshapen, for it means the crippling of thought?

. . . 27 . . .

To anyone who has begun to realise the supreme significance of what we call Meaning, nothing can be more striking than the signs and symptoms on all sides of the gradual rising of a wave of interest in the highest link between mind and mind. One thing is certain: the subject of "significance" and of the comparative failure of established means of expressing sense or meaning,—import or intention—is "in the air". One can hardly take up a paper, a review or a magazine, without discovering that. Among so many cases, it is difficult to choose: but for instance we have the discovery supposed to be made that the earth-waves, long and short, which, in their monotonous sequences and phrases, had baffled us so long, were the symbols of a language. "A language, I say, for we have no other word, but a language far transcending all spoken languages in directness and simplicity. . . . In the light of this new and obvious scheme of expression, the invention of the alphabet, whereby the activities of the mind of man are tied down to the foolish noises that he makes with his throat and teeth and lips, seemed to me the clumsiest of mishaps ":[15] and the similar discovery of " Albigo, a language . . . discovered, as the result of years of research, to exist already, and everywhere, as the base, the common principle, of all known languages, and . . . extracted, in its original simplicity, from the overgrowths which time and separateness have allowed to accumulate upon it. Albigo: the tongue which all men speak unconsciously: the universal human tongue ".[16] Then we have Wallace [17] on " Expressiveness in Speech," and the answer in "Baby-Talk of the world":[18] the "Quarterly Review" [19] on the " Art of Translation ": an excellent article by Eucken [20] on philosophical terminology: many articles on the possibilities of " style " as exemplified in Robert Louis Stevenson, Walter Pater and others: one " On an Author's Choice of Company ":[21] another on " The Genesis of Expression ":[22] the suggestive article in which Olive Schreiner says " The Taal has made the Boer in 200 years ":[23] and innumerable passages containing complaints of ambiguity even in the ablest writing not only in philosophy but in science.

These last cannot be dealt with here; but if only a few of them were put together they would effectually dissipate the curious delusion that the man of science lives in a paradise where none but plain, fixed, consistent and scientifically valid meanings can enter. We should see that the doorkeeper is sadly given to slumbering at his post!

. . . 28 . . .

When Lord Rosebery said the air must be cleared, his words applied beyond the world of politics to a sense becoming every day more urgent and more articulate, that everywhere the atmosphere is misty and over-charged with misunderstanding : that positions when not actually false are more or less falsified by mutual misconception fostered by many things, but more especially by the inveterate obscurities and confusions and the often archaic limitations of language. And what he says of Robert Louis Stevenson [24] " that he never was satisfied with any word which did not fully embody the idea that he had in his mind, and, therefore, you have in his style something suggestive, something musical, something pregnant, a splendid vehicle for whatever he had to say ", point in the same direction.

The limitations of language, do we say? Yes; but we seldom think that in great degree language is of man's making and man's mending and man's marring; that it is *we* who are obscure and confused and limited, largely because of our attitude towards expression and because of the absence of early training in the subject.

. . . 29 . . .

Of course it would be absurd to say that there are not plenty of other reasons why we should be obscure, confused, inconsistent. But just for that very reason, just because when all is done and said, most of us are sure to remain quite obscure, confused, inconsistent enough; just as, clear the air as we may, there will be an unfailing supply of haze and fog to hinder sight and breathing, it behoves us all to see that we don't leave what needn't be left in the air to blind and choke us. That at least is " common sense ".

. . . 30 . . .

Again, if it be answered that much which vitally concerns us could never be put into words, it may be fully conceded that it is so. But to repeat what has already been said, some of the " incommunicable " is dumb because it is below the level of speech, whereas some at least is so because it is as yet above that. In truth Expression, in the largest sense, ranges from the quivering of a mollusc to developments which we can work for without being able yet even to imagine. At least let us make a start in this direction. For the true principles, applications, methods, aims of Education are also "in the air". We are seeking on every side for a method "by which teachers may teach less but learners may learn more".[25] From many points of view the theories and the practical systems which now compete for our acceptance are discussed; and there is no doubt that the principles of Comenius, Pestalozzi and Fröbel's "Kindergarten" are gradually inoculating, directly and indirectly, the teaching world. But if we are to bring out—to educe —the best in the young: to make the most of such little wits as they may have by using such little wits as their teachers may have, we must begin by knowing more about meaning, about sense, about significance: we must learn to act together and in full accord on the questions which are most of all significant. For here too, while we wrangle the children are wronged.

. . . 31 . . .

The present "rage" for illustration of every kind everywhere and on every scale is owing to the same sense of the comparative failure of writing to which Prof. Flinders Petrie gives such paradoxical expression. Pictures help the reader—or ought to help him—to interpret the flat, monotonous type. But unluckily the very writing which most needs such help—that which deals seriously with the most difficult subjects—is just that which cannot be "illustrated" in the literal sense. But there is another significant tendency nowadays—the tendency to use diagram. Now you find this in places where even twenty years ago no one would have dreamt of looking for it. Why not apply the same principle more widely; why not call in the aid of indicative symbols, marginally or in the text itself? Let us learn to give writing something of the colouring of the "lecture" and the "speech"; and acquire typographic or pen-gesture, as we have already acquired mouth-gesture. If we are tempted in this and similar cases, to plead that however desirable the emancipation of language from its obsolete swaddling clothes may be, there is no hope of breaking down the hard crusts of custom and prejudice, let us remember what has happened in other cases, *e.g.*, in the journalistic world, where we learn that ".... as commonly happens in cases where restriction has been founded upon prejudice and usage rather than upon solid reason, as soon as a breach had been made the whole line of resistance collapsed at once". Here also we may reasonably hope for this result, since there is certainly no section of the community not vitally interested in some aspect of the question.

.   .   .   32   .   .   .

It is interesting to hear of the efforts constantly being made to remove the "dreadful monotony" of the deaf-mute's speech, the last being apparently an adaptation of the "musical flames". But we never seem to realise the "dreadful monotony" of *reading* even the finest poems as we are forced to do in writing or printing. Neither in handwriting nor in type have we a hint (except in the clumsy "italics" which almost mock our need) of the intonation, the pitch, or the timbre of the verses. All is one "dreadful monotony", as of colour, so of line—which must never show the faintest curve—and even of interval, except in the breaks.

between sentences and the effect of punctuation or dashes or dots,—poor things one and all when compared with what the voice gives us! But the eye even more than the ear craves endless variety, innumerable shades of colour and of tint. Both crave tone. Of course imagination may endow the barest symbol with all these glories. But if that be enough: if we are never to need or to be given more indication of the poet's sense than the dreadful monotony of the deaf-mute's speech and the written thought, why not have a strictly symbolic instead of a representative Art? Why should not a gallery consist of framed symbols like art-words, composed of art-letters,—like the printed page: all else being left to the imagination of spectators? Here a representative of Symbolic Art gives us the true answer. Mr Watts' claim [26] that a work of art should be raised to the level of the highest effort in poetry, suggests the falsity of that "impassable gulf" between the two which we assume: and on both sides the hope may be allowed that "a vein of poetical and intellectual suggestion is laid bare which may be worked with more effect by some who will come after".

. . . 33 . . .

The following anecdote [27] curiously illustrates what long custom has done in making us contented with the "dead level" of all written thought. "A man's life had been saved by the beautiful surgical skill of a successful laryngectomy. When health had been restored (the doctor) proposed to his patient the insertion of an artificial larynx, so that vowel-tones, or true voice could be added to the whisper that necessarily resulted from the absence of the vocal cords. This apparently highly desirable thing was done, but the tone, of course, was uniform; there was no change of pitch possible to the mechanical larynx, and expression, modulation, timbre — everything that makes voice pleasant and more than useful was absent. The man could speak, convey ideas perfectly, but when he tried to give emphasis, nuances, shadings, diverse meanings, and especially when he tried to express emotion, anger, or resentment, there was only the monotonous drone and squeak of the intolerable machine. Nothing could control the convulsive laughter of surgeon and assistants. The poor man's indignation sought outlet in speech, but the very words of wrath were turned to outrageous absurdity by the infernal device. In a spasm of ebullient rage he tore the mechanism out of his throat, cursed the man who had saved his life, and is probably running and hoarsely whispering invectives at him still. He never came back ".

Possibly in time we might learn to accept the "dead-level" in voice too. But why should we? And why do we in writing?

. . . 34 . . .

Since the above was written, Prof. Mahaffy has suggested, in his admirable article on the Modern Babel,[28] that at least we might begin by gradually and tentatively distinguishing by accents *thóugh* and *toúgh*, *plágue* and *águe*, according to any system which may be found most simple and convenient; and justly remarks that a paragraph at the beginning of the Grammar would be enough to explain it. Thus we should be starting a whole generation on a path which might lead a long way in a needed direction.

. . . 35 . . .

Mr Herbert Spencer[29] has well put the advantage to be thus gained, and insists that the comparative force with which simple ideas are communicated by signs shows what a hindrance to thought language really is,—as we are content to leave it, I would add. "To say, 'Leave the room', is less expressive than to point to the door. Placing a finger on the lips is more forcible than whispering, 'Do not speak'. A beck of the hand is better than, 'Come here'. No phrase can convey the idea of surprise so vividly as opening the eyes and raising the eyebrows. A shrug of the shoulders would lose much by translation into words. Again, it may be remarked that when oral language is employed, the strongest effects are produced by interjections, which condense entire sentences into syllables. And in other cases, where custom allows us to express thoughts by single words, as in Beware, Heigho, Fudge, much force would be lost by expanding them into specific propositions. Hence, carrying out the metaphor that language is the vehicle of thought, there seems reason to think that in all cases the friction and inertia of the vehicle deduct from its efficiency; and that in composition, the chief, if not the sole thing to be done, is, to reduce this friction and inertia to the smallest possible amount". But a "vehicle"—unless it is, let us say, a hearse or a water-cart—need not suggest its contents at all: whereas if a word or phrase does not suggest some meaning, it is no Sign at all and therefore not language, which is nothing if not significant. But indeed in all the metaphors used for language we miss the idea of Meaning as distinct from both thought and expression and yet common to both and their primary value. And when Meaning—really conscious Intention—may not be there: when we doubt if it is well to talk of the "meaning" of gathering clouds or falling leaves, there is still something which is indicated, denoted, or implied to us by all that happens. What is that something? We look out of the window: we see something: we speak, "naming" what we see: but the "sense" of the words we use is not our thought itself but a link between that and language. They are inseparable but they are not identical.

. . . 36 . . .

This ought to be made clear in all literature. The day will surely come when every serious work will begin with a glossary of the sense or senses in which the pivot words used, the words on which the author's thought turns, are to be taken: and obviously these senses should never, if it can possibly be avoided, traverse one firmly rooted in the general mind. If this were done, such glossaries might after a while be collected together, and the comparative value of the various usages in securing clearness and expressiveness, be shown. This would make a most interesting as well as practically useful book. As it is, no criterion is ever applied: words like Authority, Imitation, Activity, or Nature, are used at the sweet will of individual writers; but the only result is greatly increased labour for the reader, who has to let go the "meaning" the writer has imposed upon him for the moment, as soon as he reads something else.

When a writer does this he compels the reader as it were to "walk by will" as in locomotor ataxy: whereas to master his thought and assimilate his sense the reader's attention ought to be free to master the thought expressed and not distracted by constant effort to dislocate habitual interpretation. If a writer were expected as a matter of course to begin by telling us how he means to use his leading terms (which is *not* quite the same thing as defining) he could then be criticised from the point of view of comparative significance: we could ask, has he increased or diminished the expressive power of language? Then also his context would be criticised and analysed: is it ambiguous or inconsistent, or is it corroborative and illustrative? Context would thus be relieved from the heavy burden of defining now thrown upon it. How often we forget that poor context is as much enslaved by its dominant words and phrases as these are interpreted by their context! Context after all mainly gives back what it receives from a writer's leading terms or phrases.

. . . 37 . . .

But we owe more than this to Prof. Mahaffy's timely protest. He points out what we so unaccountably forget. "There was a time, not many centuries ago, when any man who chose to learn Latin in addition to his mother tongue could converse easily with any other educated man in Europe. There never was a better practical solution of a great difficulty. By keeping up as the medium of communication a dead language, if we may so term a language freely spoken, but no longer the mother tongue of any European people, all difficulties of international jealousy, which are now the greatest obstacle to a solution, were evaded". And whatever the defects of Latin in wealth of delicate shades of distinction, it was justly valued for its grammatical and logical purity and consistency, and for the simplicity resulting from the absence of "that exuberance of flexions and of particles which makes other great languages so difficult to learn". And later there was a time when French might have taken the place which Latin, for many reasons, failed to keep. That perhaps can hardly be regretted even by French scholars; as it seems to be admitted on all sides that French, while specially adapted for some purposes, is almost useless for others in comparison with English or German. Even that master of lucid expression, Ernest Renan, admits that "the clearness and tact exacted by the French, which I am bound to confess compel one to say only part of what one thinks, and are damaging to depths of thought, seemed to me a tyranny. The French only care to express what is clear, whereas it happens that the most important processes, those that relate to transformations of life, are not clear; one only perceives them in a kind of half light".

. . . 38 . . .

But though attempts either to invent or to

impose a common language would be as futile as the schemes of Bishop Wilkins (1688) or of the inventor of "Volapük", there is no reason why we English should not begin seriously to increase the advantages which our own language already has over others. "Our grammar is very easy", says Prof. Mahaffy: "our grammatical forms very few and simple: our spelling is the great obstacle. For a long time it has not represented our pronunciation with any approach to consistency or accuracy. . . . The real and only object for the present generation is to accustom the vulgar English public to a certain indulgence or laxity in spelling, so that gradually we may approach—I will not say a phonetic, but—a reasonably consistent orthography. For then every foreigner will find his task lightened; he will have some chance of learning English from books; any violations of use he commits by over-phonetic spelling will not be counted to him as a deadly crime against our language. And then in a short time, in spite of the jealousies that will arise, the British tongue, like British gold, will probably pervade the world".

This is a better as well as more reasonable hope than Bishop Wilkins gave us in his " Essay towards a Real Character, and a Philosophical Language ".[30] Indeed that good man began by assuming that " Adam in process of time, upon his experience of the great necessity of letters, did first invent the ancient Hebrew character ". He took a position less open to dispute when he complained that in our Alphabet the vowels and consonants are huddled together without any distinction, " whereas the vowels and consonants should be reduced into classes according to their several kinds ". This was indeed a " common sense " and practical proposal. Why has it been entirely ignored ?

. . . 39 . . .

As to the Spelling question, there are welcome signs that our patience with our own absurdities is beginning to give way. When scholars like Prof. Mahaffy, Prof. Earle, Prof. Skeat, Dr Abbott, are already showing up the almost grotesque anarchy which, when some " phonetic " fad is aired, we defend as if our language was spelt as consistently as the Latin, the " sensible " man to whom Sense and economy in time, brain-work, temper, have their true value, may take heart and hope to be allowed to come to his senses without being " ploughed " or ostracised for doing so. For reform in this direction urgently needs to be initiated in the world of true scholarship. We have plenty of jarring and ignorant vulgarisms already; every day adds to horrors like "phenomenal" for "exceptional"; and if the man in the street is to be left to supply our needs and provide us with reformed spelling, the remedy will be worse than the disease; we shall lose more than we gain.

. . . 40 . . .

Happily the *Times* itself—that stronghold of literary conservatism — has invited letters [31] pleading for (in every sense) a more sensible state of things; and admits in a leader that the present system is wasteful and unprofitable, that it occupies youth at the most receptive time of life to the exclusion of matters much more important, and that nobody is a gainer by the rigour now in force.

These are significant admissions. They do not point, however, either to some arbitrary and mechanical substitute for the present convention, or to individual license in spelling, which would terribly increase the burden of the reader, already too great. They really point to a keener and worthier sense of the value and a more adequate treatment of the whole question of Sense, and how best to convey it. They really imply the introduction throughout the whole course of education of systematic training in the art of being significant with voice and pen, and conversely the art of discerning and interpreting "meaning".

. . . 41 . . .

In the *Times* correspondence, Dr Abbott asks [32] whether it is not time to give up the "wasteful, arbitrary, and often erroneous attempt at uniformity", and urges that "a reasonable tolerance in these matters would be something more than a boon to schoolmasters and schoolboys". Prof. Earle [33] goes even further. He thinks that we need only take notice of orthography as we might take notice of penmanship,—that is, at the point where it ceases to be presentable. Well, the two undoubtedly stand on nearly the same ground. In both cases we have what assists, or what hinders, quick and accurate interpretation. But fixity in spelling we are told " is a denial of the first principle on which spelling ought to be governed", and thus lends force to recurrent clamour for revolutionary phonetic change.

Prof. Skeat indeed thinks it quite impossible to regulate spelling. " The one great principle in all cases of doubt and dispute, is that every man shall make his own laws, and it is not likely that argument will be listened to or even permitted ". As to the dipthong, there is, he declares, no such thing in English. And as a fact the *Times* now prints " medieval ".

.   .   .   42   .   .   .

But the general acceptance of a phonetic revolution, as a writer in the " Forum "[34] on "Spelling Reform" rightly insists, is to the last degree improbable. Any such attempt would ignore the great value and power of " the spiritual atmosphere which breathes through our language and literature". It is comforting to find an American—who is generally more ready with his changes than we are—appealing with evident respect to this as " a sentiment that has grown up in us as all sentiments do, not by reasoning, but by a complex process of association and habit"; and fully aware that " it has struck its roots deep down into the literary consciousness,—the deeper, perhaps, in proportion to the depth and richness of that consciousness ".

And it is encouraging also to find another American "speaking of Webster's unsuccessful effort to create a new language 'made in America'", saying with approval that "'Language is not a toy or a patent machine, which can be broken, thrown aside at will, and replaced with a better tool, ready-made from the lexicographer's shop. He had no conception of the enormous weight of the English language and literature when he undertook to shovel it out of the path of American civilisation. The stars in their courses fought against him'".[35] We must hope that this enormous weight may be, when a truer start can be made, transformed into an equally enormous momentum, and prove as irresistible as it was before immovable.

· · ·   43   · · ·

The difficulty is thus to make a beginning. which Mr B. Smith (in the "Forum") suggests should aim at reform not *of* but *in* the language. At present spelling reformers are deservedly classed as "cranks" who would play havoc with the historical, the spiritual, and the literary sense. But he points out that in variations already found in dictionaries, and in innovations started by influential writers, we already have the beginnings of a movement which ought to "result in the vast simplification and rationalizing of our language". Thus he hopes we should in the course of years " slowly eliminate all the gross absurdities from our written speech". The essence of such a hope, however, would lie in persuading those who already see that "there is certainly nothing more contemptible than our present spelling, unless it be the reasons usually given for clinging to it", to use so far as they can the "simpler forms which have the support of any good authority and are most in accord with existing analogies and the historic and philological standard, thus gradually habituating the public to better ways". But this appeal gives only a fresh illustration of the urgent necessity of first of all imbuing, even saturating the young mind with the sense of the crucial importance of Meaning: of securing that the child shall grow up with his attention constantly recalled to this as the vital point of all study and the condition of all success in thought, work, and life. Let him be brought up to understand that half his elders' puzzles have arisen from their not having been thus trained; and when he too is grown up he will be quite competent to solve for himself spelling and cognate problems which affect the expressiveness of language.

. . . 44 . . .

Among recent instances of discussion by public men of questions of expression and its conditions, it may be interesting to cite Mr Chamberlain.[36] He declares that the complaint that shallow praters are preferred by the average audience to men of real ability because they have a certain fluency of speech is unreasonable, because the remedy is in our own hands. "The power of clearly expressing what we know and what we think may be learnt as any other branch of knowledge, and those able and experienced and judicial men of whom the critics speak are better able to learn it than anyone else, because as they have most to say it is easier to them to say it". But in the first place where is the would-be student of Significance to go for his training? Is he to gather it for himself as best he may from the writings of the masters of "style", or from the rules of Logic or Grammar, or from the maxims of Rhetoric, or from Essays like Schopenhauer's on the Art of Controversy, Sir G. C. Lewis's Use and Abuse of Political Terms, Holyoake's Public

Speaking and Debate, and the like? If he does, most assuredly he will find that these and all other available sources of information or text-books of method will only touch on the subject here and there in a secondary way, and never reach its centre or probe its roots. What he wants is a teacher who has brought together all that these, and other forms of the study of expression, can give; and can impart an ordered as well as a concentrated result under a new heading,—let us say, "Sensifics", the Study of Sense.

For surely he will not find that as a rule those who have most to say find it easiest to say it. On the contrary the greatest minds are often those who complain most sadly of the failure of words to express adequately all their thought, and of the failure of the ordinary reader to follow them, even where words do seem to have sufficiently served them.

. . .   45   . . .

It will surely strike us some day as amazing that we should have trained our children—or professed to do so—in everything except the first thing needful, and left the royal power to express perfectly and the imperial power to interpret consummately, to undeveloped natural gift. "Let no one say", says Prof. Raleigh,[37] "that 'reading and writing come by nature', unless he is prepared to be classed with the foolish burgess who said it first. A poet is born, not made—so is every man—but he is born raw. Stevenson's life was a grave devotion to the education of himself in the art of writing.

'The lyf so short, the craft so long to lerne,
Thassay so hard, so sharp the conquering.'

Those who deny the necessity, or decry the utility, of such an education, are generally deficient in a sense of what makes good literature—they are 'word-deaf', as others are colour-blind. All writing is a kind of word-weaving; a skilful writer will make a splendid tissue out of the diverse fibres of words. But to care for words, to select them judiciously and lovingly, is not in the least essential to all writing, all speaking; for the sad fact is this, that most of us do our thinking, our writing, and our speaking in phrases, not in words. The work of a feeble writer is always a patchwork of phrases, some of them borrowed from the imperial texture of Shakespeare and Milton, others picked up from the rags in the street. We make our very kettle-holders of pieces of a king's carpet ".

.   .   .   46   .   .   .

To care for words lovingly, to choose them for the beauty or spiritual value of their form, sound, or associations, is indeed "not in the least essential" to all writing or speaking; but to care in another sense, to remember what Cornewall Lewis told us of the too easy poisoning of the wells of converse; to care also that groups of words — phrases — should be fitly chosen and combined, *that* is essential to all true speech. A patchwork of phrases will never give the royal carpet of sense which all language ought to represent. As to single words, even in this very passage, can we defend the " poet born *raw* "? Would anyone suppose him born cooked—like the defaulter's accounts? Certainly better to cook accounts than to cook poets! However, here a new defence might be set up. How many cases we have like the "impertinent" which ought to be but isn't the negative of "pertinent", the "impassable" which is far from being the negative of "passable". So it might be plausibly denied that cooked was the converse of raw. Still, the "raw" poet is hardly worthy of the use in such a context of a writer of this calibre.

. . .   47   . . .

Prof. Croom Robertson complains [38] that "there is an approach to a philosophical Malapropism in the indiscriminate use of the terms" Instinct and Intuition. But is there not, in fact, everywhere an approach to Malapropism in the use of important words in more than one sense when we have, or easily might have, distinction; and when a context, itself *partly from the same cause* ambiguous, is our only means of determining which sense? And so slight a difference might in most cases avert it! Just the difference which in spelling, punctuation, or pronunciation, does already bless or ban. One tiny jot, one minute tittle of indication would be enough, and the world of Meaning would shine out in a translucent starry sky, of which, in our present blur and fog, mirage and Jack o' lantern, we get but rare and fleeting glimpses. Strange indeed is our inconsistency herein! So rigid about the letter and so lax about the spirit: so careful of the petty points of fashion, so careless of the great points of import: so jealous for the sanctities of convention, so tolerant of the desecration of the inner shrines of speech: so fastidious on what signifies less, and so indifferent on what most of all signifies,—Significance.

We do indeed in this matter strain at a gnat and swallow a camel. When a book is seriously and worthily written to expose the actual state of things and the contrast between what easily might be with what is, we shall rub our eyes; we shall ask whether we are dealing with wild nightmare or with sober waking fact.

. . . 48 . . .

As to "misused words", about which we often see letters to the newspapers, they would demand a dictionary to themselves. Only unluckily most people think other people's usage is the wrong one: "orthodoxy is my doxy" here too. And all sorts of tests are applied; some people protest against a new meaning, some against an old one; some against one derived from slang, some against one derived from the laboratory. Some appeal to history, some to grammar: in short the "Modern Babel" is nowhere more conspicuous than in our very attempts to emerge from it. The question, what really is misuse? seems to want settling first. Nothing can be misuse which increases our resources, nothing which gives us a fresh distinction or a fresh aspect of things; and on the other hand, nothing which tends to economy or consistency, nothing which involves more wealth or more concentration. Everything is misuse which tends to poverty or debasement, which crushes thought within outgrown limits, which kills or stunts the growing points of mind, which silences the whisper of a dying memory or sacrifices as trivial or antiquated some pearl of great price; everything which blurs the lines that map out without enclosing or obstructing the mental world: above all, everything which makes for confusion and anarchy, cruelly defeating the end of the splendid gift of speech.

But this is itself a poor attempt indeed at setting forth a thesis which needs, if we would do it justice, the best powers of the highest minds.

. . . 49 . . .

An amusing instance of belief in Grammar (in the narrowest sense of the term) as the infallible panacea for all forms of obscurity or ambiguity, is supplied by Cobbett in his ingenious application of elementary grammatical lessons to the purposes of a political partizan.[39] He claims to show us that "even very learned men" have published not only what they did not mean but the very reverse of what they meant: and in this it must be owned he seems to have succeeded. He attacks Addison, Dr Watts, Dr Johnson and the great Judge Blackstone himself.

It is as he says " truly curious, that Lindley Murray should, even in the motto in the title-page of his English Grammar, have selected a sentence containing a grammatical error; still more curious, that he should have found this sentence in Dr Blair's Lectures on Language; and most curious of all, that this sentence should be intended to inculcate the great utility of correctness in the composing of sentences!" Now we must suppose that Lindley Murray, to say nothing of Judge Blackstone and the other celebrities whom he unsparingly indicts, had given some careful study to Grammar. Yet Cobbett assures us that " Grammar, perfectly understood, enables us not only to express our meaning fully and clearly, but so to express it as to enable us to defy the ingenuity of man to give to our words any other meaning than that which we ourselves intend them to express". Poor Lindley Murray!

But indeed poor Grammar is being more or less "given away" at the hands of her own votaries. Mr Sweet, *e.g.*, tells us [40] that the obstacles and difficulties in the way of a rational Grammar have taken years to conquer. Few, he says, realise how unsettled Grammar still is. "In some grammars the Definitions of the parts of speech are literally nothing more than quibbling etymologies". He taxes the existing terminology with being confusing, ambiguous or defective. He rejects "phrase" altogether "as a grammatical term, because of the endless confusions that arise between the various arbitrary meanings given to it by different grammarians and its popular meaning". As for the study of English language and literature, "until our whole system of teaching these subjects and examining in them has been radically reformed" we can hope for no advance. From the present point of view we may warmly welcome this protest.

. . . 50 . . .

Meanwhile in a true sense nothing comes to him who waits. We have been waiting for many ages for a vigorous tackling of the language subject,—a long pull and a strong pull and a pull altogether,—and of course we are little if any "forrarder". At least let us provide the rope and get hold of it.

.   .   .   51   .   .   .

Make friends of the mammon of the press. Strike fresh veins of metaphor: discover new metals, new gases, new rays of illustration; and the press will in its own interest gladly give them currency and *imprimatur*. The bus conductor and the games-man (we want the equivalent of "sportsman" in the "hunt and shoot" sense; we have already borrowed it for the moral sphere, and it there now means "chivalrous"), and the "par" man, will still bestow endless colloquial or journalistic words and phrases upon us. But we shall exploit *him*, instead of as at present his exploiting *us* and calmly imposing his "phenomenals", etc., upon his betters.

.   .   .   52   .   .   .

At present we have Language *as she is spoke*, —and worse, as she is wrote,—and think we can hope for nothing better. Even the Talker in his Millions may be taught the A.B.C's of Sense, and may discover that more order in his talking means a saving and a help. Even the writer of the cheapest Journalese may learn that more fitness in his writing means advantage. At present much is said and written merely as a pumping to meet leakage as in a crazy ship, or as a shoring up and propping of a crazy ill-built house.

. . . 53 . . .

We find a handle and a spout and then explain that there is an impassable chasm between them. Exactly: we are looking for handles or spouts to fill up the interval with. So also we can't make head or tail of the world we live in. Naturally, since it does not happen to have either,—in any sense.

. . . 54 . . .

We say when we lack something that we are without it. But we never say when we have it that we are within it!

"You'll have to do without it, do you hear? It's wanted for the marketing", said the Farmer to his boy. Now "it" was a pony; and the boy felt sure that after all he didn't want to be like the lamb which lay down with the lion— only within him. So he promised he would do well without the pony: and presently he went off to the stable, saddled it, found the hounds near by and had a jolly gallop. When he came in he found his father in a fine rage, and was told he might go without his supper. So he went off to Jenny the maid who was just going to serve it up. " I'm not to have supper outside *me* another minute, Jenny ", says the boy: " Father says I'm to be outside *it;* so give it me now, for I'm that sleepy I must tumble in at once ". So she gave him his supper, and he turned into bed and went fast asleep. But next morning the Farmer raged worse than ever and thrashed his boy, who resolved never to try and make sense out of words any more, but to chuck them about like other people into the rubbish heap, and pick them out when he wanted them. For, says he, if we are to mean "inside" when we say " within ", and not " outside " when we say " without ", where does the sense come in ?

. . . 55 . . .

I won't believe in anything which I can't feel, grasp and hold, said the evolving Man as he sat talking to the Overseer of evolution. But you'll have to, was the answer. Natural selection will see to that, and you'll be eliminated in a trice if you don't look out. Look out ? why, what is that? asked our bewildered ancestor, who hadn't yet grown any sense to speak of except touch (or the temperature sense). Well, you'll soon have to believe what you smell and yet can't touch, then you'll have to believe in what you only hear and can't even smell or taste: lastly you'll have to believe in what you can only learn by *looking out*, *e.g.*, in the sun and stars.

We are slow indeed in learning this lesson, and still grotesquely insist that any truth "beyond our grasp" shall not exist for us and that we won't be interested in anything which we cannot "touch". Away then with the astronomers! And away with the artists too: for even they give us the blue heaven and the sunset glow which we can never "grasp". Evidently, like our friends the worms, we have got no eyes.

. . . 56 . . .

People who have lost their senses — are "insane". But senses are just what they have kept. It is their right mind which they have lost.

. . . 57 . . .

"You have taken leave of your senses—you are out of your mind!" cries Mr Brown to Mr

Smith when the latter has ventured to remark that it was surely time that language took a fresh start and overtook our other advances and developments. "Certainly", answers Mr Smith. "I beg leave of my senses to see, hear, smell, taste, and touch, to say nothing of further privileges which science tells me I possess in that line; and as leave is granted, I take it and use them. As to being *out* of my mind, that is what most people insist on being. But I prefer to be *in* mine instead of having it inside me, if we must have the one or the other". "Don't talk more nonsense than you can help", growls Mr Brown, much disgusted. "Excuse me", says Mr Smith, "I won't talk more than I *cannot avoid doing*, if I am to talk as you do: for what I *can* help and mean (that is, intend) to help too, is not the nonsense which the 'man of sense' now talks".

But Brown as he goes away in a huff, fires a parting shot: "What on earth does it signify how we put things?" "It signifies what *we* signify, and that is what most 'matters' in the world", Smith calls after him: "but as yet, in our boasted speech we are like the famous Deputation, and though we signify many, we don't signify much!"

. . . 58 . . .

There is a pregnant truth in the saying that [41] "we have just emerged from a period of wrinkles and paint, during which we are told that age knew everything and youth nothing"; and that "the explosion into nonsense of nine-tenths of all we were taught at school and college has given our children a terrible weapon against us". But it is also true that "in this direction, at least, the breeze that goes before the dawn of a new century is already blowing". It is in that surely coming reign of the Young —of life in its spring—that we may look for a new growth of Expression. The same writer speaks of the signs of truth in his heroine, "dwelling not in a deep well but in clear water, as it were, open to the sky". So shall truth dwell in a wider sense and in every honest man of us, when expression shall learn more perfect loyalty to Truth, its rightful lord. Until then, it can hardly be said with truth that "what is hit is history, what is missed is mystery". For we "hit" much that is not true history at all, while we "miss" still more that is.

. . . 59 . . .

Opening one of the great Reviews [42] at

random, one comes with growing frequency upon passages describing the rise of something very like linguistic anarchism, or at least the revolt of the unbearably oppressed against all rule.

For instance, speaking of the "erratic evolutions" of a modern poet, the reviewer finds it "hardest of all, to assent to his somewhat capricious estimate of the value of words". They are sometimes to him "mere sensuous sound values — sometimes symbols deeply weighted, myth-laden—and often he uses them to express ideas.

The unsympathetic reader stumbles blind and irritated among the wreckage of the dictionary, and only the sympathetic need hope for treasure, for to know which of the three values attaches to any word or words the reader must be intimately in key with the mood of the moment". The authority of Humpty Dumpty,—representing broadly, as we have seen in "Symbolic Logic", the author of "Alice" himself,—is supposed to be appealed to "in the conflict between the author's sense of style and his contempt of sense":—

"'When *I* use a word', Humpty Dumpty said, 'it means just what I choose it to mean—

neither more nor less'. 'The question is', said Alice, 'whether you *can* make one word mean so many different things'. 'The question is', said Humpty Dumpty, 'which is to be master, that's all. . . . They've a temper some of them—particularly verbs, they're the proudest; adjectives you can do anything with, but not verbs—however, *I* can manage the whole lot of them! Impenetrability! That's what *I* say'".

But after all Lewis Carroll and his apparent disciples are clearly on the side of the angels in the great alternative of language. Only by breaking up our shameful content, if it be even by explosive methods, can we hope, they must argue, for a thorough and really epoch-making revolution.

As we stumble blind and irritated among the wreckage of our fetish dictionaries, themselves, from another point of view, the laborious victims of the irrational despots of language—use and custom;—the "betrayal of sense by sound" may be the trumpet note to summon us away to a fairer city. There "the power of making us see a picture" may become the power to make us aware of new worlds of truth and beauty to which at present we are not only blind but virtually dead, because the ways between us and them are choked and piled with rubbish, or broken down into yawning gaps and pitfalls for the unwary pilgrim.

. . . 60 . . .

What is the greatest charm? Indefinable.

What the highest beauty and goodness? Unspeakable.

What the superlative of everything? Indescribable.

And we might add: what is the ultimate value of all we can experience or know? Inexplicable.

What in short is *all our best*? Inexpressible.

But how ludicrous to say that this must be always, everywhere and to all, the irrevocable, unalterable, final law! To the babe of a few months nothing is speakable. To the babe of a few years, very little is describable, still less perhaps is definable: while its attempts at explanation are irresistibly funny. But from the first moment it *expresses* however "unconsciously" what it feels and wants. We have to grow as it does in power to express. And we have to grow as it does in power to interpret.

. . . 61 . . .

As one is alternately startled at the littleness

of man in the immensities of the universe, and at the greatness of man who can know and appraise this contrast and therefore in some sense must transcend it, so one is alternately amazed at the little power of expression man has as yet attained, and at the possible (and we may hope future) powers which he reveals when he speaks of truths beyond words, inexpressible verities, unspeakable goodness, and tells us of experience and feelings which cannot be expressed.

. . .   62   . . .

Whenever one hears or sees it said, "We have no word for" this or that, one wonders at the curious way in which we impose another law upon the decalogue and say, Thou shalt not express what is best worth expressing and thou shalt never make the word more expressive nor expand the sense of "word". Whereas for many who think thus, the "law" was fulfilled in the coming of the Logos which we are forced to translate *Word*: happily perhaps, since at least we are thus exalting the idea of word into a truer place.

. . .   63   . . .

We can never hope to learn our own limitations: in the first place we have no microscope, in the second place we have no telescope, of power enough to reveal them.

. . . 64 . . .

We ought not to submit for a moment to the lack of a needed word: we have only to awake to the awareness of our own enormous power in the matter, and the absurdities of our attitude of contented straws blown about by every puff of linguistic wind, and we shall find no more docile servant than language. It must be trained as we train eye and hand; not mechanised but quickened and developed; its precision that not of dead machinery but of living Sense.

. . . 65 . . .

"Now a dispute once took place between Mind and Speech as to which was the better of the two. Both Mind and Speech said, 'I am excellent!' Mind said, 'Surely I am better than thou, for thou dost not speak anything that is not understood by me; and since thou art only an imitator of what is done by me and a follower in my wake, I am surely better than thou'. Speech said, 'Surely I am better than thou, for what thou knowest I make known, I communicate'. They went to appeal to Pragapati for his decision. He decided in favour of

Mind, saying (to Speech) 'Mind is indeed better than thou for thou art an imitator of its deeds and a follower in its wake; and inferior surely is he who imitates his better's deeds and follows in his wake'".

(Satapatha Brahmana, Vol. XII., Sacred Books of the East, p. 130.)

But as Pragapati's words died away there appeared a third pleader who said, "O Pragapati, I think that I also have somewhat to say in this matter. For my name is Sense and I am before all else the value of all Mind and all Speech". "What thou sayest is truth", answered Pragapati. And Mind and Speech both welcomed him and said, "Verily, Sense, to be without thee is the greatest misfortune which can befall us and we beseech thee therefore never to leave us". "I will consent", said Sense, "but only if thou, Mind, and thou, Speech, will promise never again to dispute as to which is the more excellent, as though either were of value without me. For thou, Mind, art useless even to thyself without expression in some Sense; and thou, Speech, art but gabble unless Mind has filled thee with my treasures".

66

The present development of civilised language is neither natural, nor controlled and rationally intentional: it is arbitrary in the bad sense and capricious, casual, incoherent, chaotic. There is nothing gained in a barbarism which is not even picturesque, in a clumsiness which is not even forcible, in a poverty which keeps the starved thought silent, or in the synonymy and metaphor which lead to simple waste of distinction and to fallacy and "bull". What then is a natural development? In the early days, as can be plainly seen, development was along the lines of real need and best supply; each need as it arose with rise in scale, was supplied appropriately and congruously and used consistently by common consent. No doubt there were lapses and failures and abuses in plenty, but if they had prevailed, if language in earlier days had been the waste-paper basket it now is, into which any thought refuse is carelessly cast, to become the speaker's and writer's vade mecum and to clog and choke his thinking, we should not have the splendid speech-treasure which we so grievously waste and misapply. We are quite alive to the absurdity of the

Baboo English, but much of our own compared with what it might be is really little better. What is our indictment of the Baboo? Ludicrous incongruity, chaos in selection,—no *sense* of fitness. In that matter we all live in glass houses; or if a few dwell in stone secure, it is due to sheer force of genius; as a self-taught Rembrandt or Beethoven would have been.

. . . 67 . . .

It must be remembered that already the French are far ahead of us in delicately discriminative turns of expression. "How many of us", asks Mr Morley, "who claim to a reasonable knowledge of French, will undertake easily to find English equivalents for such distinctions as are expressed in the following phrases — Esprit juste, esprit étendu, esprit fin, esprit delié, esprit de lumière? These numerous distinctions are the evidence, as Stewart says, of the attention paid by the cultivated classes to delicate shades of mind and feeling. Compare with them the colloquial use of our overworked word 'clever'. Society and conversation have never been among us the school of reflection, the spring of literary inspiration, that they have been in France. The

English rule has rather been like that of the ancient Persians, that the great thing is to learn to ride, to shoot with the bow, and to speak the truth. There is much in it. But it has been more favourable to strength than to either subtlety or finish ". Now it becomes English, that Mistress of the linguistic lands as of the Seven Seas, to prove herself worthy of her great Speech-mission and of a language which already has more potential powers than any other in the world.

. . . 68 . . .

R. L. Stevenson's biographical sketch of Fleeming Jenkin is suggestive of Sense developments. "All dogma is to me mere form", wrote Jenkin: "dogmas are mere blind struggles to express the inexpressible". As we are, yes: but not as we might be! He goes on, Stevenson tells us, to say that while he thinks nothing in religion "true in the scientific sense", he thinks the religious view of the world the truest. But forms of truth, of all things, are those which God hath joined most perfectly together: let us no longer put them asunder by our falsifying words. Fleeming Jenkin "had a keen sense of language and its imperial influence on men; language contained all the great and sound metaphysics, he was wont to say; and a word once made and generally understood, he thought a real victory of man and reason. But he never dreamed it could be accurate, knowing that words stand symbol for the indefinable". Here "accuracy", "definition", stand not for the living but for the "dead" mechanical: and in this sense it is profoundly true. "Somewhere in mid-air between the disputants like hovering Victory in some design of a Greek battle, the truth hangs undiscerned". Yes: because the sense and the significance of life have never yet been pressed home in our childhood as they might be, and we must hope shall be.

. . . 69 . . .

Meanwhile the venerable Hobbes,[44] the "father of English Philosophy", was of another mind, as indeed many of us are still. To him "the light of human minds is perspicuous words, but by exact definitions first snuffed, and purged from ambiguity; reason is the pace; increase of science, the way; and the benefit of mankind, the end. And, on the contrary, metaphors, and senseless and ambiguous words, are like ignes fatui; and reasoning upon them is wandering amongst innumerable absurdities;

and their end, contention and sedition, or contempt". But Hobbes himself (followed, strangely enough, by Mill and Taine) supposed that we *mark* before we signify; whereas our expression is first a Sign and only afterwards becomes a mark. And other writers of equal eminence waste this useful distinction entirely; and use sign or mark indifferently.

. . . 70 . . .

We are told that the eye distinguishes far better than language does. Then let us begin at once to level up! For if we cannot go far with the invisible at least we ought to be ashamed to fail with the visible: that at any rate should be expressible. Again the psychologist tells us that the language of exclamation and gesture might have been developed: might have become much more fitting than it is: as it is we are apt to make ourselves ridiculous with gesticulation. Yes: just as probably the earliest speakers were often "ridiculous" to the more stately silent ones who "said nothing" but conveyed much by a raised or pointed fore-finger, or by an eloquent look or movement. To them the growing speech must have seemed (as to some taciturn races, families, individuals now), to be undignified gabbling and cackling. It really was once jabber and literally "jawing", as we still hear it called. So, when we more fully take up our heritage, it may still be that as the first speech was sure to be confounded with the chattering and gibbering of animals of the monkey and magpie order, so gestures more worthy of human dignity than any we have now will be liable to be confounded with the gesticulation of the more excitable races, as also the first expansions of our vocabulary may seem to us contemptible jargon. And we are ourselves so stiff and monotonous in our attitudes and movements while speaking, that we hardly realise how much we tend to confound the lower with the higher types of oratorical or dramatic action. French and Italian gesture is generally almost acrobatic. On the other hand, it is often true that "an Englishman speaks as though his words had wings and flew about in the air".[45] But it ought to be natural to apply to gesture, attitude, facial expression, emphasis and intonation, the same commendatory epithets which we bestow on the greatest writing and the finest acting. Charm and grace, vivacity and vividness, imperious lucidity, brilliancy and even splendour, haunting and appealing rhythm, breadth and grandeur, majestic sadness, stern or gracious dignity: terms like these ought to describe not only "style" in language but "style" in its setting of expressive gesture. "Speech is a school. Every language is a persuasion, an induced habit, an instrument which receives the note indeed but gives the tone. Every language imposes a quality, teaches a temper, proposes a way, bestows a tradition: this is the tone—the voice—of the instrument. Every language, by counter-change, replies to the writer's touch or breath his own intention, articulate: this is his note".[46] Mrs Meynell observes that though much has been said of the "note", less attention has been given to the "tone". These again are words which apply as much to gesture as to writing, where they are purely metaphorical. Meanwhile it is significant that a man's *expression* means gesture, mainly facial: and not speech or writing.

. . .   71   . . .

The current phrase "point of view" is itself an indictment. Why not a "world of view"? We want a solar system of view. If we had this we should then see that, instead of trying to crush oppositions, a better plan would be to try and understand them and carry them on further, and see what is their outcome. It may be that instead of trying to refute the opposite man we ought to try and explain him to himself.

"When the universe speaks the discussion is closed". But even short of the universe, Man may attain to a power of language which shall close many barren discussions.

. . .   72   . . .

What seems most wanted is the evolution of an international court of voluntary appeal on all questions of expression. This would be far more effectual than any Academy, while free from its objections. In cases of senseless fashion we find consensus easy enough. We all go to the glazier for our houses, we all crowd into the same boat, wondering that it promptly capsizes and drowns us; and almost fight to be tarred with the same brush. Yet when it is a question of acting all together for a mighty effort to get clear of smashed glass house and sunk boat, and of making a bonfire of the tarbrushes, then of course nothing can be done. But would it not be real common-sense to get some common consent to a common sense for language? We are striving for common consent to a voluntary Court of Arbitration for international questions: and in time, if such a Court may be, not imposed, but evolved as government and law have been, and become binding as they are in civilised nations and as "custom" is in barbarous countries, we may be far more hopeful about an International Court of Linguistic Arbitration. For we are such unwilling victims of linguistic war! And there is no glory to be won on *that* field, no jealousies to appease or ambitions to satisfy.

.   .   .   73   .   .   .

The Thinker was once called the Seer, or the Magician and the Wizard, then the Prophet, then the Philosopher, then the Mystic; whereas now he is proud of being called the Critic. Let us hope that in the future he will be called the Interpreter or the Translator, and that there will be "chairs of Interpretation". Yet even then words express but poorly the rising hope that libraries of meaning wait to be read and rendered. Even now, one man will teach and another learn more in half an hour, and over one page or one "example", than others in a month. It is quality that we want, and we are getting mainly quantity, masses of fact, expanses of theory. More central points in investigation, more touch with the core of our subject, that is the need.

. . . 74 . . .

The Medicine-man must become the Meaning-man; the Soothsayer must become the Sense-sayer. We want language farms and gardens, and Scholarships of Expression, Interpretation and Translation. He who expresses most and in the best way: whose definitions are the most adequate, his descriptions the most graphic, his explanations the most lucid, his epithets the aptest: he who brings us most out of least and in least time or with least brain-expenditure: he who most discards intellectual padding and phrase-making, and yet captures and holds his hearer's or reader's attention and interest best, making attention most interpretative: he who can state a thesis in most dialects of thought, and point out best where translation is impossible and why,—will graduate in sense *in a new sense.*

. . . 75 . . .

It seems strange to read [47] of Quintus Ennius "the first of the great Roman poets" occupying himself diligently with questions of language and even an elementary system of shorthand, and to learn that even in his time, chiefly owing to his own genius and industry, "the literary capabilities of the Latin language made a very great advance". When may we hope for a new Ennius? And more: when shall we see a new Lucretius,—a thinker who on the one hand can throw himself back into prehistoric conditions and pierce the dim horizons of the illimitable past till he finds the speechless Man, and on the other can penetrate and read the future as Lucretius did, in advance even of Newton and Lavoisier? But think a moment: our Lucretius would be dumb. He would open great eyes full of truth ready to be born: but it must have an Expression as full of new Life as itself. How could he bring it forth in the stunted and wizened body of speech with which we are content? Lucretius rose not only to great heights of thought but to the "utmost perfection of language". And we are still almost where he was, except indeed that in some ways we have lost what he had. We must hope for a Thinker like another classical giant to give us a new world of Expression; one of whom it shall be said, as it is said of Cicero,[48] that "he created a language which remained for sixteen centuries that of the civilised world, and used that language to create a style which nineteen centuries have not replaced, and in some respects have scarcely altered ": that indeed he did " what Lucretius, with his far greater philosophic genius, totally failed to do—created forms of thought in which the life of philosophy grew, and a body of expression which alone made its growth in the Latin-speaking world possible ".[49] And he again was followed by one of whom it can be said that his method of expression " almost amounted to a new human language". Thus when we protest that nothing can be done to exalt language into greater fitness, we are put to shame by men who saw that their true work in life was to mould their native language into something higher than till then had been known or possible. The conditions of course were totally different. Things possible then would be out of the question now. True: but the converse holds also. Things impossible then have been made possible by the invention of printing, by the enormous diffusion of writing, by the ease and quickness of communication, by the ever increasing tendency in mankind to combine for purposes of civilization.

76

But let us turn to an even more striking witness [50] to what has been actually achieved, and what therefore we may confidently hope for again on a scale commensurate with our modern resources. There has been an "Ennius" of the East also. The East in which,—until Japan shattered some of our most familiar assumptions—we have supposed that nothing was ever changed or ever developed: which was entirely guiltless in our eyes of that restless energy and enterprise and love of novelty of which we are alternately proud and ashamed: India itself, the land where all life is still ordered on immemorial lines and where it is "always afternoon", has put us to shame in this very matter of attaining a higher standard of expression than could have been dreamt of a hundred years ago. What Ram Mohun Roy began in 1790 as a lad of sixteen, has become a "vast and vigorous growth" not merely in native literature but in its linguistic resources. Literary dialects have been actually created. "Varieties of human speech never reduced to writing have been furnished with alphabets and printed types", and now for the first time supply vehicles for the complex problems of philosophy, science and modern thought. In the case of Bengali, this wonderful beginning of what was virtually a new world of language, "starting on its career under the impulse of a master-mind and under the formative touch of a master-hand", has since been "developed into a strong and dignified language for historical, philosophical, and religious writings. In the process it has freely borrowed from the inexhaustible storehouse of ancient Sanscrit and has equipped itself with a terminology for scientific works from the English". As to Japan, she is even now giving us an object lesson in the rapidity with which a language may widen its boundaries and absorb and assimilate new elements.[51] "The influence of English has effected modifications in the native tongue making it richer, more flexible, and more capable of expressing the new forms of thought created by the discoveries of modern science"; and this extends even to its grammatical structure. And yet there may well be a deep truth in the remark that "English itself has been a demoralising influence". There are many reasons why a language so rapidly borrowed and so entirely alien to the one which absorbs it, should be this. But the main reason of all is the general

Grains of Sense

lack of control over the activities of language, the general absence of belief or interest in its potential greatness.

. . . 77 . . .

With such facts as these, then, staring us in the face; and when, even in our own early history, it has been possible to speak [52] of "the gift of a new power to the English tongue" within the limits of a single reign, shall we still go on saying that the language-question is hopeless? Do we really suppose that we could never interest the public in general, or parents and schoolmasters, or even the leaders of philosophical and scientific thought, in the urgent need of further developments in Expression? True that most of these movements have been started by individual genius. And may one whose gift is to make the dumb to speak and the deaf to hear and the blind to see what now is neither spoken nor heard nor read because we declare that it is " beyond words ", arise and draw us irresistibly by the force of his personality to see and to hear and to read those things which have been hidden from us because they could not be in any wise expressed or represented! But even so why should we wait for the One Man? Let us hope that a group of men will soon at least prepare the ground for him. Many fruitful ideas forming themselves under the surface but never finding public expression as things are, will rise to the light and silence the riot and clamour of the mob of senseless talk which dazes and wearies us, if it does not lynch our thought. It is a true saying [53] that there are vital points on which no one can now think as he could have thought once, however hard he tried. But there are other vital points waiting for the breaking down of walls and the bridging of gulfs which have been the prisons of our thought—of truth which could never have been thought before because it could not be worthily expressed. "The things you can't say", observes Prof. Dicey,[54] "you soon cease to be able to think";—or, you never become able really to think. And if it be true in any sense that "the man who adds a pleasure to life is a king, while he who removes an anguish is a god", what shall we say of one who helps to teach us what the Word may be and bring to us, who gives us fresh worlds of Significance? In words which have been used in a somewhat different context, the conditions of language "call for a palingenesis, a new birth, in which man shall once more rouse himself from his sordid acquiescence in the established fact, and realise the wonderful heights and depths of his own nature ". [55]

. . .   78   . . .

What an era the word Prig marks. The aphorism that delighted the last and preceding generations now seems sententious: for the modern saying is rather pregnant by reason of paradox and gives us small shocks—it is more or less "sensational". But the sententious has only quite lately become related to the priggish. It used to be the terse, the pithy, the significant.

. . .   79   . . .

When we are superlatively stupid and cannot understand the thinker at any cost, we like to have the best sort of excuse—that which makes us feel superior. "You are not luminous, my dear friend" we say, as the man said to the sun when he came out from grubbing in the dark cellar. Yet even the effects of a drug may baffle our poverty-stricken and outgrown vocabulary. When, in an experiment, Dr Weir Mitchell tells us [56] that he had a certain sense of the things about him as having a more positive existence than usual, he adds, "it is not easy to define what I mean, and at the time I searched my vocabulary for phrase or word which should fitly state my feeling. It was vain ". We will hope that it will not be vain much longer, and that it may become possible with a regenerated language " to describe the hundredth " part of what we may experience under special circumstances. It is rather mortifying to realise that as Nansen has usefully reminded us, the Eskimo "never utters a syllable of abuse, their very language being unprovided with words of this class, in which ours is so rich ".[57] It is to be feared that English would not yield the palm to Norwegian in this form of wealth : and we might well renounce some of these odious riches while acquiring worthier possessions. Perhaps when we have attained more power of expression, we may learn better what " luminous "— and what " colour "—may signify to us.

. . . 80 . . .

We probably think that so long as we confine ourselves to good plain homely words like "light", in use by all and understood in the same sense by everybody, we must be safe. It would be obvious nonsense to talk of a " pitch-dark " room full of light. " Invisible light" is clearly a paradox and surely a bull: we might almost as well adopt the famous remark that the moon made everything as light as a cork. What man has named "light" or its equivalent in all languages, is that which can be "seen" and which makes "seeing" possible, and is nothing else whatever. Here at least there is no ambiguity. It seems hardly credible that the scientific world is at a lower level in the use of this word than the popular world. It actually writes about black light, Le Bon's "lumière noire".[58] And while Dr Lassar-Cohn very truly says[59] that the Röntgen rays "are not light because we cannot see them", Prof. Thomson talks[60] of the "invisible ultra-violet light"; and says "by light I mean transverse vibrations propagated with a definite velocity"; and thus includes electric "waves" which traverse walls and bodies, etc., of nearly a mile of densely populated streets. Prof. Newcomb told us nearly four years ago[61] that we had much better banish the word "light" from physics. He suggested the very simple term "radiance", which as he says, seems just what we want. And he pointed out that the derivatives would be readily formed. The verb "radiate" would mean to emit radiance:

Radiometry would mean the measure of radiance : while instead of talking of transparency (or translucency, etc.) we should speak of the *transradiant* or *transradious*. Others wrote to plead for the same distinction in other cases, and one writer suggested [62] *irradiate* instead of "illuminate". But Lord Kelvin's decision on the matter ought to make further discussion needless. In his "Six Gateways of Knowledge" he says that "if we distinctly define light as that which we consciously perceive as light . . . we shall be safe. There is no question that you see the thing : if you see it, it is light". When the frequency of heat vibration exceeds a given limit, "it is not light since we cannot see it ; it is invisible ultra-violet radiation . . ."

The discovery of the X rays has made the distinction more valuable than ever. Yet we see that it is entirely ignored. Even the Christmas Lectures for children at the Royal Institution for 1896-7 were on Visible and Invisible light, as if it was expressly desired by Science that the children's minds should become hopelessly confused as to the meaning of one of the words now clearest to them!

81

And we must not forget another very important sense of the word "light" which would be falsified by this change of usage. We have been crying for ages "more light, more light". Now the answer is surely come. It is a command to change our prayer and to cry "more sense, more significance": and light will follow. But then this is the light which is visible and exists only within the visual range. Just as "sound" carries hearing, so "light" carries seeing. At present mental light seems one of the truest metaphors we have. Let us husband, not destroy our resources.

82

Some of the most instructive cases of the Epithet which is first suggestive, and then question-begging, may be seen in the late American Presidential Election. On the one side we had Sound Money (tacit converse, Unsound money); on the other Free Silver (tacit converse: Locked-up Silver?). The epithet "anarchist" has been the decisive term of the American election, and now the anarchists and their denouncers are apparently living together in great peace and comfort. The "honest dollar" again was a potent phrase: but it has been pointed out that an appreciating dollar is as "dishonest" to a debtor as a depreciating dollar is to a creditor. Clearly on both sides it it was largely a war of phrases. The Spectator said [63] of Mr Bryan that "if ever man forced his way to the front by sheer command over words it is he"; and that "he has to perfection the art of phrase-making, the art which enables the orator to lead men by words as one leads a horse by the bridle". On the other hand we have a well-known writer in the *Times* answering a question about the "Ratio" by the statement that he does not agree with the American advocates of "sound money", "*even as to the meaning of the words*". Of course the parties to a controversy all have their own language: the pity is, that this is also all the language we others have: we who are not partisans, and want Expression for the great issues of Life and the great worlds of Knowledge and Imagination.

. . . 83 . . .

What is wisdom? Coleridge's "common sense in an uncommon degree"? And what is an aphorism? Is it, as Mr John Morley tells us,[64] "good sense brought to a point", "having" as Bacon puts it "a point or edge whereby knots in business are pierced and discovered", or Cicero's saltpits from whence to gather and sprinkle salt? Anyhow the "wisdom of life" which true maxims contain certainly cannot be, as Mr Morley says, the true *salt* of literature, if those (prose) writings are "most nourishing which are most richly stored with it". Salt may give savour, but that it should nourish is indeed a new and startling ideal!

. . . 84 . . .

But indeed metaphors are often terrible things in present use. Take the various metaphors of consciousness, to be found in an article in "Brain" by a distinguished thinker.[65] After laying down the distinction between consciousness as a Knowing and an Existent, the author illustrates it thus: as

1. a *Field*
2. an occupied *Point of view*.
3. which *embraces* (all being) and is
4. (by implication) a *Substance*
5. a *Stream* of many currents
6. which becomes a *Panorama* and a
7. *Ground*.

This Field, this occupied and embracing Point

of view, this Substance, this Stream, this Panorama, this Ground, has *Layers* understood as time-sections in its time-stream (so it now *possesses* a time-stream?) and it has a *Mechanism*.

As things are, all writers are more or less "in the same boat". Though we do mostly see that incompatible metaphors used together of anything defeat each other and deepen darkness, yet we go on using them and even introduce more. Mr Laird Clowes, wishing to bring home to us the idea of a given encumbrance, described the Mediterranean as a millstone round the neck of England. The answer has been, "But *you* would substitute a minor planet", *i.e.*, an immensely greater encumbrance. But what if the substitute had been described as a stream or a cloud or a wall? At once we are confused; all is incongruity, and we are better without any metaphor at all. . . . Lord Shaftesbury says of Locke, "Innate is a word Mr Locke poorly plays on. The right word, less used, is con-natural. For what has birth or the progress of the fœtus to do in this case?" What indeed? But the same question might be asked in many cases. What are "mixed metaphors" but bulls?

85

As to the herds of these devastating animals which overrun the fair fields of literature and toss and gore and trample us not only in Ireland but wherever English at least is spoken, (has anyone seen or heard of a foreign bull?) startling you by appearing where you least expect them, one of the brightest hopes of the future "Sensifics" would be its power of rendering them harmless and even useful by confining them to zones where on the one hand they would still yield sport for our budding legislators, and on the other give us directly or indirectly good honest beef which now we often cannot get. For serious bulls—sometimes called paradoxes—and what is more, serious puns, which have no other name as yet, might often be serviceable as object-lessons in the dangers which lurk in all attempts to convey some valuable meaning not already worn threadbare by mechanical repetition in "hackneyed" phrase Meanwhile let us consider a few specimens encountered in unlikely places. It is sad to have to begin with Darwin himself. But what else than a bull is his title "The Descent of Man", when the whole object of the book so designated was to substitute for that idea its converse, the Ascent of Man? No doubt the metaphor Descent might still be used, but for Darwin only in a secondary and therefore changed sense: while he actually speaks of "descent from the lower forms of life". But he does not stand alone. For instance one scientific expert tells us [66] that in terrestrial plants are "the roots of the animal world",—whereas neither an animal nor a world has anything analogous to roots; while another [67] announces that "the advance in every section of chemistry during this century, and especially during the latter half of it, has literally been by leaps and bounds"!

. . . 86 . . .

To pass from science to philosophy, the downright bulls of metaphor which we find in writers of the front rank sheds a curious light on the way in which the illustrative powers of language are running to waste on all sides. The first duty of an illustration is obviously to illustrate: but such illustrations as the following illustrate nothing but the need of a more delicate figurative touch and a more sensitive analogical conscience: if we say that just *because* an "ultimate reality" is "the primary truth upon which all our intellectual and practical life is built, it must be that which casts light upon everything, and upon which everything reflects back light",[68] the value of the comparison is at once destroyed. Things don't cast light because they are buried under buildings as foundations! Again, if we use the metaphor "above" for our "highest" aspirations, and with Xenophanes "look up" to the expanse of heaven and declare that "all is one": if in the earliest days men were "led to raise their eyes above the special forms of nature to the over-arching heaven" in a "lifting of the spirit", we must not go on to speak of their literally raising their eyes *and* their spirits![69] Nor, "when we turn to the practical life" need we ask, "where is the religious zeal whose heat is not hostile to light",[70] since obviously nothing analogous to heat can be hostile to what corresponds to light. This author himself deprecates "imaginative symbols that are opposed or indifferent to science", and demands the "fullest satisfaction of the requirements of scientific criticism";[71] so that he must equally desire the fulfilment of the conditions of clear expression.

Hume's putting casual instead of causal

succession is, we are told by one of his ablest critics, "to put the cart before the horse, not only metaphorically but really";[72] a curious use of the "real"! Another distinguished writer speaks of "two voices apt to overhear the third";[73] an experience almost worthy of the old couple who were so proud of having been married on the same day. When another (a logical) writer asks, "instead of there being no break or seam in Nature, is not its whole structure composed of breaks or seams—which only do not appear such because they are small and familiar",[74] we wonder how a structure can be composed of breaks or seams except on the principle of the Irishman's coat, which was a big hole with a few bits of stuff hanging to it. Another tells us that "unlimited extent in time and space can be constructed".[75] How do we set about constructing that which has no limits? These propositions sound rather like the bull quoted by Mr Bosanquet[76] when showing that you cannot prove that parallels never meet. "In order to do so, you would have, like the Irishman, ' to be there when it did *not* happen'".

. . .   87   . . .

From philosophy and logic we plunge back

(antithetically?) into politics, and learn that [77] "it has become a stand-up fight between two immemorial tendencies of mankind, the desire to stand still and the wish to go forward, and between these two parties there is no abiding place. The men of the future are those who will go the whole way with one or with the other". With the one which is standing still for a stand-up fight? One of the neatest of these cases is Mr Stead's,[78] when after comparing the country to a great Atlantic liner, he likens a certain Bill to knocking a hole in the hull below water-line, and worse, to shifting the ship's centre of gravity so as to make capsizing a certainty. Then he ends, "This is not metaphor. It is simple, sober, serious fact". One more instance of what Dr Murray calls the "self-centred proposition" (as long in use before "Irish bull"): the *Times* in a leader once told us [79] that "to simulate mock wonder, mock anger, mock derision, and mock contempt in a speech delivered amidst the cheers and the plaudits of a great popular audience, that really feels the sentiments which the orator who is addressing them feigns, is a comparatively easy business to any practised rhetorician". To simulate mock anything is certainly a notable feat.

. . . 88 . . .

As to the Schoolmasters and Inspectors of Elementary Schools, let us quote the "Journal of Education";[80] it reads in the "Schoolmaster" that certain reports "'will presently be relegated to that hermetically-sealed oblivion which lies in wait for those who deal with the esoteric operations of the schools'". As the Journal remarks, "bottled oblivion lying in wait to devour the pedagogic writer is a fearful wild-fowl"; and besides that, demurs to "silent explorations" which "evoke an echo"! And yet "the staff of the 'Schoolmaster' represents the very pick of the profession". Well, attention to these matters has formed no part of their own training.

. . . 89 . . .

When shall we grow—or educe—a figurative conscience? In one sense it is only too possible to have one. It would be useful in some cases to consider how far a given type of conscience —say the political—has gone over from the actual to the metaphorical. Conscience may perhaps need to be classified. But the question is, whether we do not all more or less need to develop a figurative conscience, to be more conscientious in the use of figure. How many of us feel an inward prick when we have used a handy, popular but yet dangerous metaphor, or have used a safe one in the wrong way? Who, when the audience applauds, the critic praises, the public buys and reads, thinks of the poor victims of his brilliancy? Who indeed believes in their existence? The temptation is always to ignore the implications of metaphor. It is taken for granted that no confusion could be caused by or traced to them. And then there are the words which in their literal sense contradict their accepted sense. A man may say, I will neither say that I can't grasp it or that I cannot make head or tail of it: I'll say simply, You must make me understand it. But my friend, that is just the difficulty. You *are* required to *under*stand questions, whereas you will insist on *over*standing them, and persist in trampling them into the soil and then wondering that they are obscure or muddy. This is true " superstition ". You are always demanding the grounds for this and the solid support for that; whereas in understanding, the subject-matter is " above " you, and you look up to it.

Only, beware of erecting walls on your horizon and a roof on your sky,—your eyes, the physiologist will tell you, are focussed to "infinity". What you really understand is ipso facto over your head; what you never can understand is the well-based statement. Do you say, but what is over my head I must *grasp* or I cannot see it and follow you? Well, to follow me you must get rid of those relics of a pre-historic plant-stage of your existence, the roots of your thinking which you so "highly" value. But even then, as you see only with your fingers, you must renounce all knowledge of sun, moon, and stars, as they are neither tangible or palpable, and pull down your speculative observatories with their visionary astronomers. Nay the very bird which soars and sings is out of your reach, and as on the wing is non-existent for you. No wonder then that you "fail to see" and "have yet to learn" the A. B. C.'s of those questions which perplex or distress you or excite your scorn as futile. You have started with a grotesque chimera; facts refuse to be compared with it, to square with it, or to comply with its conditions even in the broadest sense; they require to be described by images which are valid and appropriate *so far as they go*, thus generating in other minds a pictorial impression which will stand test. But even when we have a relevant image, like "understanding", we have "yet to learn" that it is sometimes the fashion to use it upside down, which may perhaps account for some muddles! When the poor facts find themselves described in figures which throw "light" upon them instead of "dust" into our eyes, and are no longer compelled to make guys of themselves in our masquerades of imagery led by the very lord of misrule, we may re-discuss many questions with renewed prospect of fruitful answers. As we are, these are hopeless, because they depend on unconscious, involuntary, inherited myths lurking at the initial stages of our thinking :—sirens which "land us" poor shipwrecked flounderers in a dead-lock ?—no; for even *that* has a handle on one side and a key on the other as every locksmith would tell us; and our blind alleys have neither key nor handle, any more than a retina on which an "image" may be flashed, a nerve along which its message may pass or a loophole through which our further way is discoverable.

. . . 90 . . .

Mr Literal was a useful citizen and a respected public servant, although he had inconvenient limitations. For instance, as often as he sat down to dinner, he insisted that he was in the Chair and called for the Minutes. Nothing would induce him to hear from his friends by post; for you don't hear, he would say, what is written: and a post don't bring letters. On the other hand he consistently declined a seat upon any Board, as in his eyes, boards, like planks, were not suited to that dignified use. Indeed Board was one of Mr Literal's many bugbears. For while it was really nothing but a long narrow piece of timber sawed thin, it pretended to be all sorts of things which it obviously couldn't be,—as we see in the case of a frugal board, a card-board, passengers on board or falling overboard, a board-school and a sea-board parish. In Parliament his deference was always paid to the Member who happened to be speaking and never to that most silent of members who, to his indignation, was called Speaker. And here the subsequent proceedings were sometimes of interest. But he was always ready to serve the "rightly-named" speaker (or writer) with points of emphasis; and these indeed seemed naturally to belong to him.

. . . 91 . . .

Mr Literal's immediate connections were somewhat homely, and belonged to the Fact family, who are the Browns if not the Smiths of the practical world. But he claimed cousinship with the powerful clans of the Real and the Actual. Thus we see that Mr Literal had an immense sphere of usefulness of his own, and helped with his cousins to furnish one of the most convenient of contrasts,—that between his own and the aristocratic, poetical, but sometimes flighty and fanciful Metaphor family. The Metaphors belonged of course to the most illustrious of races,—that of Illustration; though unfortunately some of their scions were black sheep and devoted themselves to obscuration (to smudging their fellows), instead.

Now Mr Literal, like the rest of us, had his weak point; and that, alas, had been found by a certain Miss Metaphor. He fell, of course literally, head over ears in love with her; though how he did it remains a mystery, as unluckily no one was present to Kodak the operation for us, and X rays were not invented. Now it was always understood that this young lady would never admit to her society any one who could not boast an illustrative descent or a figurative character; and our friend's knowledge of this fatal obstacle to his hopes tempted him to sacrifice for the charmer's sake his ancestral integrity and self-respect. He began, at first feebly and in a half-minded manner, but soon more boldly, to climb into that high and select region of the Figurative, to which he had always formed so instructive a contrast, and of which his very existence was the needed foil. How he managed we must not ask. Some experienced interviewer, exploring our sad secrets in disguise, might reveal the process; but one thing is certain, there at last he was. And most ludicrous looked the honest creature in his borrowed skins and feathers; for all that made his value and even his dignity, to say nothing of his Sense and Meaning, were gone. The flowing draperies, bright colours, fantastic designs, fanciful forms, which were the natural trappings of the world of the illustrative, only made him look preposterous. But alas, the courtship is still going on. The evidence of this is crowding upon us; and it may not be too late to call the poor man's attention or that of his family to the fool he is literally making of himself in prosecuting his hopeless suit.

92

To take a few recent examples of his masquerading exploits, we have [81] " Ministers prating economy, and buttoning up their pockets against the most urgent demands of the public, at the very moment when they are literally flinging money with a lavish hand into the dirt ". It is to be hoped that they let the needy public know the exact hour and place of such a convenient largesse. M. Clemenceau, again, was once [82] " literally being hunted to death ". The pack was in full cry; one expected at any moment to be in at the death. M. Clemenceau's turns and twists were really curious. He led his pursuers off upon unexpected scents, or now and then turned upon them, " holding them at bay and showing his teeth ". One wonders where the French kennel is; and which of the French votaries of 'Le Sport' owns it and rejoices in the well-bred and well-trained pack and the well-preserved quarry. " With smiling face, in softest voice, almost literally bubbling over with gratitude," Mr Chamberlain [83] once " thanked the Government for the concession just made ". Do his friends now always watch fascinated for signs of the rising, say, on the tip of his nose, of the first minute bubble of the lather of gratitude?

Meanwhile when, only the other day the House "literally tied itself up in its own red tape",[84] so splendid a conjuring feat must have filled the performer with pride; and after this it sounds quite tame that once upon a time at least "Lord Robert Cecil literally fumed with rage".[85] Were the fumes asphyxiating, like the terrible after-damp of mines?

· · · 93 · · ·

But to turn from political news to other departments of intelligence, we find that an idea may be literally turned inside out:[86] while in a public inquiry on a "Trust" question[87] it was explained by a witness that a large amount of money literally went into the sea. "The walls were washed away by the sea, and thousands of pounds went with them". What a pity to have embedded the notes or coin in the stones of the wall! But millions of money are often described as literally thrown away;[88] while we never hear of their being literally fished out of rubbish-heaps again, though a magistrate tells us that the proprietors of "penny gaffs" are literally coining money.[89] Meanwhile the other day the

Grains of Sense

billiard champion "literally pulled the game out of the fire".[90] Again on a recent occasion "the President of Magdalen, who made an admirable speech, found his words literally drowned in applause".[91] It was fortunate that there was no one there to commit the unpardonable waste of literally throwing cold water upon the poor drowned words.

Certainly if a modern sea-fight may apparently leave "both men and ships literally torn to pieces, but still not blotted out, as one might have expected":[92] if the famous Umbesi impi was literally wiped out:[93] if a traveller survives being literally smothered in dust and sand:[94] or on a whaling cruise, may be for weeks "literally up to the neck in blood":[95] "if the only way of meeting the enhanced price of flour will be by reducing the consumption of what, in the most literal sense, is the staff of life":[96] if we have "forced the inculcation of an alien and a detested creed upon the Chinese, literally at the point of the bayonet":[97] if in 1585 France "was literally torn in halves between the League and the Cause":[98] if sympathy can literally grow out of self-preservation:[99] lastly, if we can make our way to Paris with our life literally in our hands,[100] then "Alice" might have spared all her trouble in exploring Wonderlands or Behind the Looking-glass Countries. And we gladly agree that it is " wiser to have a single wife than four who literally devour you ": [101] better to have no boy than one " literally all eyes and ears ": [102] and perhaps more prudent to be content even though your fame does not literally ring throughout Europe,[103] so that your only wonder is that you don't find it practising literal leaps and bounds in a Newspaper office, as even Chemistry has so successfully done in the last half century.

But enough of poor Mr Literal's romantic vagaries.

In these desperate but futile expedients we find that while he has lost a character of the highest value, what he has really gained after all is not the privilege for which he craves, but something fatal to his pretensions to be either Literal or Figurative in any rational sense : he has begun to acquire the horns and hoofs, the lashing tail and bellow—of the Bull.

EYE THE MYSTIC.

"My dear Eye", said the Hand one day, after having held a book containing sundry eloquent passages on the grandeur of Doing and Making, the impotence of mere Reason and Knowledge, and the fatuity of Criticism,—"My dear Eye, I do wish you would learn your place. Why, you can neither grasp nor make anything! Action, my friend, Deed, that is the glory of Man——" "And Progress!" added the Foot, which had stopped to listen. "You look and stare or peep and peer, and 'Behold',—you say,—'I see': and yet you never get any 'forrarder'. Do be less visionary and more useful if you can: but if not, don't give yourself airs!" "I don't" began the poor Eye: "It's the Ear that does that: I give myself Ether and Light——" But the Skin impatiently broke in: "And what do we want with your boasted 'light' and your pretended knowledge of the distant?" it scornfully asked: "surely I bring Man all the intelligence he needs, except what my friends the Nose and the Palate give. I am the best of Newsmen: I am really in touch with things, you know. Come to me for the tangible and the palpable and for feeling and sentiment: these are what Man most values!"

"Yes", they all cried to the Eye, "know your place, for you can hope to know little else that we don't give better still".

"Softly, my friends", here interposed the Brain: "mind what you're about, or I shall stop the supplies till you know your own places better". And they all trembled and were silent: but the Eye rejoiced, for he knew that though he could actually make nothing and could neither construct nor advance: though he knew Feeling only as Pain and to him its result was only tears or blindness, yet his work was dearest to the Fountain of Meaning,—Man. Greater than all other messages was his message, and deeper than any its human significance till the hour of Speech should strike.

Yet he was not elated by the Brain's rebuke of his fellows. "Be content, my brothers", he said gently to those who had derided him: "for though my vision brings truth to Man which you could never reach, yet I need you all.

Each of you must act upon that which of myself I can not even see: and my light is only good as Man lives by it both in thought and action, and above all in love ".

THE ANIMAL CRITICS.

The creatures who had too much common sense to go in for the chatter and jabber they heard man use, grew so provoked with his conceit that they summoned him to a court composed of them all.

Then said the Beasts and Birds to Man :—

" You say you 'know' this and that, and can talk and write and argue, and can reason things out and do other wonderful things with what you call your mind. But to us it is all just a jumble of noises; there is no clearness in it. And even if we do catch here and there some plain simple grunt or howl or hoot, we can't see the sense of it, or make out what it all comes to, or where's the proof, or what's the use of what after all isn't good to eat or to kill enemies with, or even to escape by. Now *do* be definite and explain all these things which you invent and use, and your axioms and grammar and so on. And tell us what you really mean by all these funny black marks on the white stuff you call paper; for we doubt if you know yourselves, in spite of all your big talk". And the like challenges resounded on all sides.

So the Man tried to explain; (for he began to be a little ashamed of having forgotten his mother-tongue of the animal world). And he began slowly; using the simplest words he knew, and combining them with the gestures which he inherited from his hearers.

But :—" You must bark plainer", says the Dog; "Do croak clearer", says the Frog; "Give me a definite roar", says the Lion; "Or a simple bellow", says the Bull; "And an unmistakeable growl", says the Bear; "And a sensible whinny", says the Horse. "No", says the Ass; "Give us a good long common-sense bray, for hee-haw's the best speech, and every creature's a donkey at heart". Here the birds chimed in. "If you can't yet even fly like us, at least you can whistle and scream, and could try to caw and crow and cackle distinctly, so that we may know what you mean". "Or perhaps", some softly added, "You could warble or pipe or coo or trill; or at any rate you could chirrup".

"Be definite", each cried in his own lingo;

"and we will hear what you have to say; but if you can't make all our noises at once in such fashion as to make your meaning plain, we shall know that your boasted 'speech' is nonsense".
"But" says the Man, "don't you know that I am further advanced than you? It is not for me to talk in a lower language, but for you to learn a higher. I too am dimly conscious of greater language which I must learn; though sounding to me as yet as my speech does to you. But I know that that is for want of a sense in me, which I hope to acquire some day. Already I can make out a little, and great is the reward therein. I mean to give my life to patient trial. For now that I have begun to understand *you* I shall soon begin to show you how to understand *me*: and moreover I shall learn the true hope of language for *me*, by mastering its true origins among *you*".

"Listen to him!" cried all the beasts and birds at once: "what arrogance in his looks and jargon in his mouth! Away with him". And they all set upon him. But there ran out a two years' baby with a ripple of crooning laughter and a babble of vague sounds. And the beasts and birds left the man and went their several ways. The babe will teach him, they said.

INTERVIEWING AN IMPASSABLE GULF.

I looked over his edge.... There he was, endlessly busy, keeping his two sheer precipices apart. For they were always squeezing together and wanting to interchange courtesies and everything else they had or were; and if once they succeeded, what was to become of him and then of the poor old universe, which, as we know, can't possibly get on without chasms that are unbridgeable? It was the growing public uneasiness on this subject which had determined me to seek an interview with the widest and deepest Gulf I could find. If I found him shrinking or shallow, a note of warning must be sounded. Why, even Mind and Matter might make it up and get married, and where would posterity be then? This was the general feeling; but I own I had serious misgivings about it all and was determined to get to the bottom of things—if indeed there was any to get to.

My first query brought a startling reply. "Yes, it's desperately hard work", said he, panting a little as he paused in his strenuous exertions to keep himself nice and yawning

Grains of Sense

for all who came to his brink. "You see I have to make believe so very much, or else I should be found out in a trice. I have to look very black and drop things into myself that they may sound faintly hollow as they strike upon my ribs, and make me seem unfathomably profound". "But after all", I ventured to ask, "why *should* you pretend and work so hard, and what would happen if you *were* passed?" "Filled up if I know!" said he (I looked my shocked feelings at such an expletive) "but you see I'm under a contract to behave as such, and my very existence depends on my carrying it out. You wouldn't have a poor respectable chasm like me committing suicide or becoming chargeable to the rates as a hopeless deficit, would you?" "Well", said I, "if you'll excuse me I think that as you *are* such a fraud, anything would be better than your trade of making people believe that the universe is split in half, and that nobody can ever get across or fill up the crack. Don't you see that if it wasn't for you people would not see double as they do, and there wouldn't be half the quarreling nor half the puzzles there are, while we should learn many things which an impassable gulf compels us to remain ignorant of?"

"That's true enough" he replied, "though you're getting rather out of my depth". (But I haven't got in! I protested). "Well, please go and say all that to the people who put me here and work me so hard in trying to look what I'm not, and to frighten wayfarers who suspect like you that any baby could walk across me if it only tried, and that my sides are always pushing hard to come together. I say, you look kind and sensible". (I blushed at the chasmical compliment and tried to look as deep and vacant as I could). "Couldn't you persuade my Company to make me into a Link? That would suit me much better, in fact I believe it's my natural vocation, and then I could enjoy being real, after being a swindle for so long. And then you see you can tell them that they needn't be afraid of things tumbling together in a mass, for even a link means that things linked are distinct. O dear, it's weary work this". And he fell to his labours again; for while he was talking he was getting to be a mere slit from the anxiety of his sides to come together. So I promised I would do what I could; and think of getting up a Society for the turning of Gulfs into Links. Please don't think I am going to make any bad jokes about games. Perhaps

Grains of Sense

the Abolition of Chasms Society would be a safer title. Abolition is generally no joke. Will you join us and sign a petition to the Purveyors-General of Impassable Gulfs to the Republic of Letters? Or shall we get up a syndicate and show them how much better it would pay to deal in Links instead?

"SO-TO-SPEAK" AND "AS-IT-WERE".

"So-to-speak" and "As-it-were" were in a great fuss one day. They could not make out why some things were dedicated to them and others not, though they came under the same category. And moreover, they had heard people protesting that analogy and metaphor were all very nice, but after all they taught nobody and proved nothing.

"What was wanted" said these people, "was to know what was really the case and to arrive at solid fact". (Now, thought our friends, as these are not acknowledged as ours, they must be literal. So, said one to the other, "Is the *case* an empty one do you think? And is a *solid* fact a block of wood or of what?") Analogy and metaphor, people went on to agree, were capital as fancy ornaments, so long as nobody took them seriously, or supposed that there could be or ought to be the smallest likeness between the things thus compared. But serious writing ought to be free of them. So poor So-to-speak and As-it-were felt very shy and small finding themselves in the awkward position of witnessing by their very existence, as respectable phrases, to the unreality of all analogy and metaphor alike. And they felt their own existence thus undermined. Indeed it was really fatal to language itself, as the very idea of meaning attached to a noise or a mark carried both analogy and metaphor in its very essence. Every word ought by rights to be dedicated to one or other of the friends. But indeed the more they thought about it the more puzzled they grew. For here were all the greatest thinkers and men of science writing big books, each from his own point of view to instruct his fellows, and these books were crammed from one end to the other with metaphorical and analogical expressions and phrases. And then if, wanting to be accurate, you went to the etymologist and philologist, they only enforced the lesson.

Every now and then a "sop to Cerberus" ("this belongs to our friend the Myth", remarked So-to-speak), was thrown to the two friends, whose names were stuck in as saving clauses ("Why, that's mine too", said As-it-were). And sometimes their various connections, Illustrations, Simile, Symbol, Figure, and last but not least, the relation they most admired and reverenced,—Parable, were invoked in order to strengthen an argument or convey an impression.

But as the discussion to which the two were listening proceeded, they could stand it no longer. They left off listening. "What's the meaning of wiseacre", says So-to-speak? "O, it's the field one finds at one's wits' end", says As-it-were. "Let's sit down in it then; for I am sure I am at mine, and the people we've been listening to seem very far afield!"

HOW TO STAND UPRIGHT.

In the nursery one day, the Needle, the Walking-stick, the Toyship, the Candle, the Hoop, the Top, and the Baby all discussed together the best way of standing upright. The Needle said "You must be stuck into something". "No" said the Walking-stick, "you must be held in a hand". "Not a bit" said the Toyship, "you must float on a liquid surface". "You'll find there's only one way to manage it", said the Candle, "You must be fitted into a candle-socket". "Much better roll along straight as quick as you can!" retorted the Hoop. "The true way is to spin so fast that you seem quite still and are described as 'asleep'", cried the Top.

Meanwhile the Baby had struggled to his legs; and after swaying backwards and forwards for a moment, proudly stood upright and looked round upon the company smiling. "You're all wrong", said he, crowing and chuckling; "for I'm stuck into nothing, held in nothing, floating on nothing, fitted into nothing, and neither rolling nor spinning! The best way to stand upright is to get on your legs, and stay there". But the others all sighed. And one whispered to another, "Yes; if you've got legs to begin with."

CHANGING VIEWS.

There was once a Planet which was always going round a moving Sun and turning upon itself meanwhile, so that "up and down" and "right and left" were ever being reversed to it, as also "to and from". And on it, there was *life*. Now this planet had a meteoritic friend, who thought that no other condition was reasonable or desirable for any mass of matter, but that of a detached and aimless Meteorite; independent of its fellows, but ignorant of the *whence*, the *whither*, and the *why* of its own course and of theirs; abjuring all "teleology" of solar genesis, and knowing not itself as really grain of sun-stuff. So the Meteorite-friend came to visit the Planet one day, after a long interval. And as they talked, and the Planet spoke of what it saw from the point it now had reached in curving orbit, the Meteorite said, "Why, you've quite changed your views since I met you last! You seem to have lost sight of the constellation-forms you used so to admire and point out to us; you seem to see the universe from quite a different position. Now therefore surely you must know 'fixed' centres, bases, or foundations as but our childish fancies, now outgrown; as I and those like me have learnt to do. And of course now you don't believe in all the antiquated notions we meteors so despise, about being 'a planet bound in an orbit round a sun' as the condition of producing something known as 'life'. You see now at last that 'planet' and 'sun' and 'life' and such-like things are but the outworn dreams of a fetish-era or a myth-stage, don't you? You see like us that the very idea of a solar system is itself a mere survival of exploded fable; and that after all we are nothing but meteorites, swarming and rushing, and jostling in the dark,—'light' too being really nothing but a fancy bred of trembling hopes and fears?" But the Planet stared. "What can you mean?" it said. "Why, how could one be a planet at all or have an orbit related to a sun, without changing one's position and one's views in ceaseless movement and in countless revolutions? I get fresh views, of course, from every point I reach in my concentric spiral orbit. And know you not that when I come again to the point where once you found me, the universe will no longer seem the same, even thence. Our Sun is wending on a way of glory; drawing his own along with him on an unknown solemn journey; leading us all somewhither in the degree of silent space. . . . And on my breast throb life and light and love, as on my Sun, with all my sun-linked brethren, I fix a stedfast mind; constant, unswerving, fearless, on the Planet's ordered way."

THE EVOLUTION OF HELIOLOGY.

The world was learning much, and thinking more, and stirring with fresh wonder. And there came to it a Teacher well assured. His sight was swift and keen, but its range was curiously limited by a peculiar form of short-sight. He could discern nothing beyond the atmosphere of earth, and thus had never seen the sun. So he reasoned with a sun-conscious organism, and sought to prove to it that the origin of all its forms of expression was earthy. "Trace them up", he said, "and you everywhere find that form-colour, motion, growth, even thought, are only transformed energies evolved by the earth. As these develop, as activity increases, as functions multiply, and as you become conscious of them and at last able to reflect upon and reason about them, you suppose, —fatal error!—that they are somehow derived from a source extraneous to the soil from whence they sprang. Thus, also, with sensations of light and heat. They both originate exclusively from the organic germ itself, or from its earth-environment. The notion that light or heat-rays come from and are due to some great 'sun' in distant space, independent of earth (though earth is dependent upon and revolves round it), is pure delusion. It would be useful to write a paper on the 'evolution of sunrayism', or perhaps of 'heliology', and to show how the ideas of a sun as fountain of light and heat and chemical force arose,—to trace back, in short, their history and genesis. For it is plain that even were there any foundation for the myth of a sun, it must be beyond our faculties of perception, as beyond our atmosphere; and the idea of our learning its constituents or movements and action, yet more of our consciously receiving its emanations and influence, must in the nature of things be groundless. It would be easy to show the natural process by which in times of scientific ignorance the heat in the earth's centre, shown in volcanic action, geysers, &c., and in deep mine-borings, the light and flames produced by friction, phosphorescence both animal and mineral fluorescence, and the diffused light of a self-luminous atmosphere, have been exalted by the infantile credulity of man into the revelations of a mighty life-imparting, light-giving atmosphere, the cause and origin of all activity on earth, and of all the rich and complex phenomena of our existence".

Grains of Sense

Here the group was joined by an egg-enclosed Embryo, which observed:—" I have just been lecturing in the same sense to my foolish brother-embryos, who persist in sticking to similarly obsolete notions about being 'hatched'. They, too, apparently inherit a sort of glorified ghost-theory, by which they flatter themselves that they originated not primarily from the speck out of which it can be proved that they grew, but from some mysterious source outside the very egg itself, forming round them what they supposed to be a mere shell, some day to be cracked and 'transcended', but which, like the atmosphere you speak of, encloses us in barriers which cannot be passed even in thought. So I explained to them that all theories which foster a craving for post-shell-cracked existence are sheer fancy; for the sooner we all understand this, the better. As you and I know, the very idea of such 'parentage' is due really to inflated dreams of our dignity and destiny, which have a morbid origin. So strong, indeed, is the tendency to carry high-flown mythological fancies into detail, that some even declare that, once outside the shell, they will acquire powers not merely to run upon the earth, but to 'cleave the skies on wing'."

The conversation was now taken up by an Orange-pip and a Wheat-grain. "We quite agree with you", said they; and the Orange-pip continued:—"I can contribute some curious facts from the experience of my own tribe. Some of us claim a subtle faculty of conception, an inward power of perception, a receptive organ of reflection, by which the wildest stories and legends are certified and taken as representing sober fact, and revealing verifiable principle. One such imaginative pip asks us to believe that it originally dwelt in a golden globe attached to what it calls the branch of a tree, and surrounded by so-called leaves—whatever such terms may stand for—and further fancies that this globe started from the centre of a corolla of fragrant 'leaves', called the petals of a flower. Not content with such a tissue of idle dreams, the pip insists that within the shrine of its own heart lies, ready to be drawn forth by the action of that very extraneity called 'sun', the promise and the potency of a plant to spring from it that shall consist of root, stem, and branch, of leaf and flower, and fruit, and thus of seed again. And it maintains that the very condition of this development is that first it shall moulder away, be broken up and die as seed in earth".

Grains of Sense

Here broke in the Wheat-grain:—"Some of us, I can assure you, go even further in their folly. They not only fancy that they are conscious of a plant-life beyond grain, but one actually teaches the 'law of sacrifice' in life through death; affirming that the supreme destiny of the wheat-grain is incorporation in a higher organism than any plant-form known. It tells us that not only are we to abandon all care for self-preservation as intact seed, to fall cheerfully into fertile soil, and there in pain and darkness waste away in order that at last, through utter dissolution, our hearts may germinate and ascend towards the light, but that corn has another 'privilege', a representative 'glory'. It may, forsooth, be ground, and then be kneaded and exposed to fearful heat; after which it may be received into and assimilated by a more complex organism, to help in forming tissue composed of innumerable cells like our own, but with indefinitely greater powers of combined consciousness and action. A fine prospect and a likely issue, truly!"

"Well", said the Pip, thoughtfully, "my friend, too, spoke of the golden ball being cut when he fell out, and its substance being taken into some organic region unknown to us, to help in building up a finer structure ".

Here the Teacher was observed to be making notes with an air of being somewhat taken aback, and was heard to mutter:—" This must be seen to. I must correct the mistaken inference that because there are no sun-rays to produce or stimulate these processes, therefore they don't exist; I must write an 'Essay on the Science of Biological Ethics', which shall show that all this really takes place, but through forces wholly derived from earth ".

A fragment of ice and a crystal of snow lay close together listening, and near them rested a particle of carbon. Said the Ice to the Snow:—" Let us take all this to heart. We used to think that if warmth came to us, it was from a sun, and if we melted, though I lost my gem-like glitter, and you your exquisite design, yet that we should find a larger life in flowing through the world in fertilising streams; nay, that beyond all present limits, we should be drawn up by the sun in wreaths of filmy vapour from the earth, returning there in life-bringing showers to aid sun-work. But clearly warmth is earth-begotten and death-dealing; we melt, and we are *not*". "Aye", sadly echoed the

Carbon; "and once I thought that, dull and uncomely as I am, I too might one day enter into a glorified state of radiance men call 'diamond', and that the many colours and the sparkling light I should give forth, would reflect the fabled 'sun' they speak of". Soon, many murmurs took up the burden both of protest and regret. All Nature seemed perversely to have given one hand to heaven and the other one to earth; from all sides came the voice,—"Behold the sun! what witness need we that it *is*?" But the Teacher smiled. "It is curious", he said, "how the growth of superstition follows the same laws everywhere. It is a weed hard, as all weeds are, to kill or root up finally. Ideas long cherished, however baseless, tend, both in the individual and in the race (through heredity), to project themselves into a sort of spurious objectivity. You will hear many declaring that they *see* the sun, and often watch with rapture its glowing, radiant disc behind the many-hued clouds, at what they call sunrise and sunset. And numbers maintain that the alternations of night and day, winter and summer, witness to this ultra-atmospheric luminary, instead of merely being special forms of a general law of rhythm, or action and reaction, as observed, *e.g.*, in the phenomena of sound. As well might we attribute to the influence of the tidal ebb and flow, the rise and fall of our own respiration! It is time that the sun-myth were finally discarded. Intelligent and reasonable beings should recognise, even though with pain, the limit of their knowledge and their vision. It is plain common-sense that we cannot know what is beyond the region of the atmosphere, or penetrate the vacant, sunless depths. Let us all be satisfied with earth!"

FINAL NOTE.

As any "grains of sense" which may be found embedded in the sections of this little book certainly point to a plague of misunderstanding which is fatally raging amongst us, the author, even apart from obvious personal disabilities, has no right to assume that its implications are unmistakably plain. But at least the drift of the whole can hardly be misconceived: and few would deny that, supposing that the nations of the earth could be brought as near together in mental as they already are in physical communication, such an achievement would mean nothing less than a new era in human thought and action.

If anyone thinks it futile to point out the disastrous effect upon the welfare of the world which linguistic barriers may involve, let him ponder well some pregnant words used the other day by Sir John Lubbock:[104] "I do not think", he said, "that at any time in the history of the world the modern language teacher has had functions so important as he has at the present day. If you look back upon the year which has elapsed . . . and cast your eyes over Europe, what do you see? You see there the six leading powers of Europe, all of them desiring to act in a certain way and with certain purposes, and yet not a single one of them daring to act, because each of them is afraid of what the ulterior motives of the other five may be. Now, that is a state of affairs which, whatever our political views may be, I feel quite sure that we all realise to be a most deplorable one in this civilisation of ours of the nineteenth century. It is just because the different nations of Europe, on the one hand, have been brought by modern means of communication so close to one another that one of them cannot act without affecting the others, and because, on the other hand, intellectually and spiritually they have not been brought so close to one another that they are able to understand and to trust one another, that we are in this terrible difficulty to-day".

He then went on to say that "the grave question which confronts us—the gravest question perhaps that has ever confronted peoples in history—is the question of whether we are going forward to the United States of Europe or backward again into a time of barbarism, from which we shall have slowly to build up a third or fourth great civilisation of the world". It may be feared that the mere acquirement of the various tongues which are dominant in what we call European civilisation would, in all but a few rare minds, consume too much time and energy to leave much for utilising the tools thus acquired. For it must include languages so difficult as Russian, and,—so long as Turkey and Egypt form part of the problem to be solved,—even perhaps Turkish as well as Arabic. But at least here we find in the mouth of one of the most practical of teachers a full recognition of the need, and an emphatic warning of a danger which we disregard at our extremest peril. The mutual deafness, dumbness and blindness which is the mental condition of our "Modern Babel", but which leaves us only too free for mutual collision, quarrel and destruction, must indeed make terribly for war, and even, through mutual hatreds thus engendered, for reversion to barbarism. As we cannot speak with each others' tongues, we cannot hear with each others' ears or see with each others' eyes; and thus the natural human jealousies and rivalries are without an equally natural corrective.

It must be admitted, however, that another view of the matter exists and cannot be ignored. It has lately found a powerful advocate in Lord Salisbury, who holds that the barrier presented to mutual understanding by difference of language has acted as a non-conducting medium for the irritating poison generated even by merely ill-natured comment. He suggests in fact that if any one language became generally understood and used, the ignorant or unscrupulous mischief-maker with his irrepressible telegram would become more dangerous than ever, and might plunge us into war over a hasty word which had roused an uncontrollable storm of popular anger.[105]

But to this it may be answered, that the

remedy keeps pace with the disease; that the power to disavow and counteract by contradiction or explanation would be correspondingly greater. There remains however the objection that words once said always leave their sting, and that no repudiation can cancel their effect absolutely, or ensure that it shall never be revived in ignorance or malice. Therefore we are once more brought face to face with the broader question. If the fomentors of quarrels and creators of discord are to be victoriously met by those who represent and make possible human civilised society and co-operation: if the forces of international law and order are to triumph over those of anarchy and mutual extermination as they have already done within the borders of each national organisation, it must be done by arming them with weapons of expression of far greater power and perfection than any yet attained. The weapons we need must be to those we now have what the modern weapons of war are to the primitive axe, spear, and arrow. The peace-maker of the future must be able to make his appeal ring high and clear over the medley of clashing interests, and his words must fly home with unerring aim and resistless force to the real " heart " of the matter in dispute. Language must no longer remain the too ready and efficient ally of moral or intellectual drawbacks in himself or his hearers.

These, however, are hopes which can only be realised in the distant future. Meanwhile, he who should do something seriously to raise the question of clearer, more intimate, more sympathetic mutual interpretation, from a mere aspiration into a working international agreement, would in the first place undoubtedly deserve, if he did not actually win, Dr Nobel's prize of £10,000 " to be allotted to whomsoever may have achieved the most or done the best to promote the cause of peace ". Few things indeed would be likely to do more to further the prospects of universal peace, than a general expansion of the limits, and regeneration of the conditions, of linguistic converse between all civilised nations. But in the second place, as already urged, he might give the first impulse to a work of unique greatness. He might be the pioneer in exploring and annexing new worlds of expression. He might be the first to give us access to much that is now still beyond the power of words to convey, and yet is often that which beyond all else needs to be expressed. He might be the apostle of a significance which would, in senses which as yet lack their adequate signs, reveal the secrets of life itself. His work would cover the whole ground of human interest, and would be significant in a sense which must itself be enriched and expanded.

REFERENCES

Section.		
5.	[1]	December 21st, 1896.
6.	[2]	Sir E. du Cane on Convict Prisons, quoted in the *Review of Reviews*, September 1896.
10.	[3]	"Use and Abuse of Political Terms".
	[4]	"Public Speaking and Debate".
	[5]	"Hume", p. 86.
11.	[6]	"Symbolic Logic", p. 166.
12.	[7]	*Fortnightly Review*, August 1896.
14.	[8]	Frazer's "Golden Bough", p. viii.
15.	[9]	*Nature*, January 7th, 1897.
20.	[10]	British Association, 1896.
21.	[11]	Leader on do., September 24th, 1896.
22.	[12]	October 3rd, 1896.
24.	[13]	"Social Rights", vol. ii.
25.	[14]	"Science", January 1st, 1897.
27.	[15]	"Human Bacillus": Prof. Walter Raleigh, *New Review*, November 1896.
	[16]	"Friend of Man": H. Harland, *Yellow Book*, October 1896.
	[17]	*Fortnightly Review*, October 1895.
	[18]	" " " 1896.
	[19]	*Quarterly Review*, October 1895.
	[20]	*Monist*, July 1896.
	[21]	*Century*, March 1896.

	[22] *Westminster Review*, May 1896.
	[23] *Fortnightly Review*, April 1896.
28.	[24] *Times*, December 11th, 1896.
30.	[25] "The Great Didactic": Comenius, trans. by Keatinge.
32.	[26] G. F. Watts: His Art and His Mission: M. H. Spielmann, *Nineteenth Century*, January 1897.
33.	[27] "Meaning and Method of Life": G. M. Gould.
34.	[28] *Nineteenth Century*, November 1896.
35.	[29] "Essays", p. 230.
38.	[30] *Works*, vol. ii.
40.	[31] December 17th, 1895.
41.	[32] December 12th, 1895.
	[33] December 17th, 1895.
42.	[34] November 1896.
	[35] *Dial*, November 16th, 1896.
44.	[36] Address to the Birmingham Debating Society, *Times*, October 29th, 1896.
45.	[37] R. L. Stevenson, Royal Institution, May 17th, 1895.
47.	[38] "Elements of General Philosophy".
49.	[39] "English Grammar".
	[40] "New English Grammar".
58.	[41] F. M. Crawford's "Adam Johnstone's Son".
59.	[42] *Athenæum*, January 9th, 1897. Review of L. Housman's "Green Arras".
67.	[43] "Aphorisms", p. 41-2.
69.	[44] "English Works", vol. iii.
70.	[45] Holyoake's "Public Speaking and Debate".
	[46] "Rhythm of Life", p. 54-5.
75.	[47] MacKail's "Latin Literature".
	[48] *Ibid.*
	[49] "
76.	[50] *Times*, April 21st, 1896.
	[51] "Kokoro": Lafcadio Hearn.
77.	[52] Green's "History of the English People", vol. i.

References 145

79.
- [53] "Recent British Philosophy": David Masson.
- [54] *Spectator*, December 12th, 1896.
- [55] *Daily Chronicle*, June 12th, 1896.
- [56] *British Medical Journal*, October 5th, 1896.
- [57] Review of "Fridtiof Nansen", *Spectator*, December 19th, 1896.

80.
- [58] *Nature*, August 13th, 1896.
- [59] "Chemistry in Daily Life".
- [60] Rede Lectures, *Nature*, July 30th, 1896.
- [61] *Nature*, November 30th, 1893.
- [62] „ February 22nd, 1894.

82. [63] July 1896.
83. [64] "Aphorisms".
84. [65] "The Philosophical Relations of Neurology": Shadworth Hodgson, *Brain*, Part 1, 1891.
85. [66] "The Origin of Land Animals": Dr H. Simroth, *Nature*, July 21st, 1892.
- [67] "Rise and Development of Synthetical Chemistry": Prof. Thorpe, *Fortnightly Review*, May 1893.

86.
- [68] Caird's "Evolution of Religion", vol. i.
- [69] *Ibid.*
- [70] „   vol. ii.
- [71] „
- [72] "Hume": Prof. Knight, p. 160.
- [73] "Locke": Prof. Fraser, p. 296.
- [74] "Distinction and the Criticism of Beliefs": Alfred Sidgwick, p. 260.
- [75] "Handbook of Psychology" (vol. i.): Baldwin, p. 242.
- [76] "Logic" (vol. i.), p. 339.

87.
- [77] *Daily News*, January 13th, 1894.
- [78] *Review of Reviews*, March 1893, p. 237.
- [79] February 20th, 1892.

88. [80] October 1896.

92. [81] *Speaker*, June 13th, 1891.
[82] *Times*, March 2nd, 1893.
[83] *Observer*, June 18th, 1893.
[84] *Westminster Gazette*, March 2nd, 1897.
[85] *Speaker*, January 5th, 1895.

93. [86] "Organic Evolution and Mental Elaboration": H. M. Foston, *Mind*, October 1895, p. 473.
[87] *Times*, March 25th, 1893.
[88] *Daily Graphic*, August 10th, 1891.
[89] Montagu Williams, p. 11.
[90] *St James' Gazette*, January 1897.
[91] *Speaker*, October 27th, 1894.
[92] *Spectator*, July 20th, 1895, p. 75.
[93] *Pall Mall Gazette*, January 4th, 1894.
[94] "Pamirs", vol. i., p. 222.
[95] *Times*, May 27th, 1893.
[96] *Daily Graphic*.
[97] "Far East": H. Norman, p. 304.
[98] Frith's Life of Giordano Bruno, p. 70.
[99] Hoffding's "Outlines of Psychology", p. 248.
[100] *Literary World*.
[101] *Fortnightly Review*, July 1895, p. 55.
[102] "Prairie Folks:" H. Garland, p. 148.
[103] Heinemann on the *New Review*.

FINAL NOTE.

[104] Address to Modern Language Association, December 23rd, 1896.
[105] Lord Mayor's dinner to Mr Bayard, *Times*, March 3rd, 1897.

www.ingramcontent.com/pod-product-compliance
Lightning Source LLC
Chambersburg PA
CBHW030332170426
43202CB00010B/1094